Money Sense

To Helen
with Best wishes
Harwood Michael

Money Sense

The
Parents' Guide to Teaching Children about Money

HARWOOD S. NICHOLS

ACROPOLIS BOOKS LTD.
WASHINGTON, D.C.

This book is dedicated to Rebecca, Susannah and their generation, who will soon be passed the torch of liberty, mortgaged though it be.

ACROPOLIS BOOKS, LTD.
Colortone Building, 2400 17th St., N.W. Washington, D.C. 20009

Printed in the United States of America by COLORTONE PRESS
Creative Graphics, Inc.
Washington, D.C. 20009

Attention: Schools and Corporations
ACROPOLIS books are available at quantity discounts with bulk purchase for educational, business, or sales promotional use. For information, please write to: SPECIAL SALES DEPARTMENT, ACROPOLIS BOOKS, LTD., 2400 17th St., N.W., WASHINGTON, D.C. 20009.

Are there Acropolis books you want but cannot find in your local stores?
You can get any Acropolis book title in print. Simply send title and retail price. Be sure to add postage and handling: $2.25 for orders up to $15.00; $3.00 for orders from $15.01 to $30.00; $3.75 for orders from $30.01 to $100.00; $4.50 for orders over $100.00. District of Columbia residents add applicable sales tax. Enclose check or money order only, no cash please, to
ACROPOLIS BOOKS LTD.
2400 17th St., N.W.
WASHINGTON, D.C. 20009

Library of Congress Cataloging-in-Publication Data
Nichols, Harwood, 1942-
Money sense.

Includes index.
1. Finance, Personal—Study and teaching.
2. Children—Finance, Personal—Study and teaching. 3. Consumer education.
I. Title.
HG179.N53 1987   332.024'007   87-24129
ISBN 0-87491-871-5 (pbk.)

Book design by Kathleen K. Cunningham
Cover photo by Neil C. Hughes

Acknowledgments

I am deeply indebted to the many parents, teachers and financial professionals who aided me in formulating the ideas behind *Money Sense*. Without their thoughts and support, the book could not have been written. I am especially grateful to John Peterman, Jim Ball, Dick Kodenski, Katherine Crawford, Warren Shimmerlik, William and Kathy Zurilla, Ruth Mascari, Jim Riepe, John Le Cheminant, Walter Whilden, Larry Hayden, Bill Joseph, John and Anne Patterson, James Johnson, Marian Randall, Steve Sands, Sharon McCarty, John Hornady, Kevin and Judy Campbell, Dick Greene, Pete Meyer, Bruce Brereton, Andrew Nichols and Emile Bendit.

To Mary White, my typist, Kathleen Hughes, my editor, and her staff, I offer a special thanks for their tireless efforts and professional guidance.

This book in many ways is the inspiration of Phil Trupp, my literary mentor, whose unflagging support has proven crucial to the project.

Finally, to my wife, Barbara, and our children Rebecca and Susannah, I express my sincere appreciation for their continuous encouragement throughout the writing of this book.

Harwood Nichols

Baltimore, Maryland

TABLE OF CONTENTS

Foreword

"Dad, why aren't we rich?"

No one can really tell parents how best to teach their children about money. Nevertheless our awareness of the importance of money in American life depends, for the most part, on attitudes developed during childhood.

This book is a collection of ideas to help parents develop in their children healthy attitudes about money.

It is for parents who are rich, poor, and in between. It answers questions about who is financially successful and more importantly why. It talks about the importance of probability in dealing with reality. The ultimate purpose of *Money Sense* is to make children more confident by telling them the truth about the world they live in.

As a trust banker I try to help families reconcile their personal circumstances with the money they have available. Often the problems I encounter stem from unrealistic attitudes, attitudes formed during childhood which result in anxiety and unhappiness.

Many American families discuss money the way Victorian families discussed reproduction. Legitimate questions are parried with cliches, or suggestions that the child, regardless of age, has no need to know. Such responses are employed because parents themselves have not thought out their answers, or even worse, want to manipulate the child by imparting an emotional or mysterious aspect to the family's finances.

I think children should be taught that political and economic forces will impact their lives, and their future success may depend on their awareness of these events. Since schools generally shy away from money subjects, their teaching becomes a parental responsibility. Like sex and religion, where attitudes are changing, parents often find themselves on thin ice when talking about money. But the ice is no thinner than that supporting their child. Parents can be prepared to pass on their own experience and at the same time develop in their children common sense instincts to capitalize on the opportunities which they will encounter. The parent can also encourage the child to understand his own abilities and their relative value in American economic life.

Beyond these fundamental attitudes, children can begin to understand the nature and purpose of our economic and financial network. Where does money come from? What is the purpose of the stock market? How is income allocated? What is the role of government? Why do people starve when America has silos full of grain?

Children intuitively ask such questions in an attempt to comprehend their environment. If they are answered with truth, they will grow to be confident and responsible citizens. If they are answered with ignorance, they will become insecure, distrustful and afraid.

Perhaps unfortunately, American children are born into a world with a dollar sign on it, and forever after are reconciling their feelings with this reality. Their basic instincts say they want it all. Their teachers say to disregard money and seek a higher goal. Their parents send out a mixture of signals which add to and compound their confusion. Money is said to be unimportant, but everything we value seems to have a price on it. If we have money we want more. Like rats in a maze, we scurry along, reacting to artificial stimuli, arriving at the end, exhausted, confused, and with the nagging suspicion that we never really understood the rules of the game; and when our children ask about those rules, we can't explain them.

I have tried to provide explanations of our economic system in terms that are easy enough for parents to use in discussing such things as the stock market with their older children, or to answer questions when they arise from younger children. I believe that when children ask questions, they are ready to hear a valid answer.

The activities at the end of each chapter are suggestions for family learning experiences, maybe not quite as much fun as going to the movies, but stimulating nonetheless. Use your judgment. When children are ready, try a particular activity they will understand. And, of course, decide how much of your family finances you are ready to discuss with your children.

Money Sense, as the title implies, presents common sense explanations of the complex concept of money in our economy. It is for parents, children, and families who would like to get the question of money in America—and their own finances—out where they can be discussed realistically and candidly. I hope this book will provoke some thoughtful ideas to help you guide your children in plotting their futures.

Harwood Nichols

Prologue
The American
Economic System

"Mom, why can't America feed all the hungry people?"

THE PROBLEM OF INEQUITY

Not too long ago a U.S. senator suggested that some of the vast grain surpluses held at government expense in U.S. warehouses be shipped directly to Africa to feed the poor. The plan's strength seemed to lie in its simplicity. On the one hand, U.S. taxpayers would be relieved of a costly storage problem, and on the other starving people would be fed. Not much different from collecting food for the needy at Christmas time.

The *Washington Post* responded in an editorial that while the senator's sentiments were well placed, economic realities precluded the implementation of his plan. The *Post* explained that dumping grain on the market lowers prices and limits future food production by making it less profitable. Imagine African farmers struggling to sell their grain to buy seed and equipment for next year's crop, only to have prices collapse because of free American grain.

Some, of course, would accuse the *Post* of being cynical in protecting the profits of well fed farmers while others starved. But the *Post* was right. The economic realities of giving away food will eventually undermine the good intentions of the moment. This ability to consider the economic realities of a situation is a mark of intellectual maturity and can be fostered in our children. Because economic factors are often expressed in dollars, they give the appearance of putting a price tag on all human endeavor. And, of course, this is true. Whether it should be the basis of how we decide things is another question. The physical reality is that the earth's available resources have to be allocated in some fashion, and economics is the method and measurement of this process.

Parents and teachers often fear that emphasizing the economic aspects of life will erode idealism. Certainly we do not want to suggest that children (or senators) should be indifferent to the hardships of their fellow human beings. But if that hardship is going to be relieved, the process should be economically feasible or their idealism and good intentions will be crushed on the anvil of financial reality. Some would argue the point, but does it make sense to feed one starving person, if in the process you create two more?

Fairly early in life parents can begin developing in their children the ability to evaluate the economic aspects of a situation. Even though few of us have formal academic training, economics is a subject that lends itself to common sense. Like a chess game it helps to think a few moves ahead to achieve a successful conclusion.

To understand the economic motivations for human endeavor is to add a dimension to your view of life, and to have a framework by which other factors can be evaluated. When Bob Woodward was unraveling the complexity of the Watergate scandal, his famous anonymous source Deep Throat constantly reminded him to "follow the money." Aside from all the political, psychological, and personal motivations, the money would wind like a tarnished silver thread through the entire maze. Not that money was the sole or even primary motivation, but it was the constant one.

College students during the Vietnam War were driven to behavior that appeared insane to their parents. The students could not understand why we were fighting the war. The waste of life seemed totally disproportionate to the tortured reasoning put forth by our government. What the students never understood was the short-term economic bonanza created by the war. As a friend of mine said at the time, everybody was making money on the war except the people fighting it. Like World War II, Vietnam gave focus to the economy, but without the economic dislocations caused by the earlier war. George Orwell predicted as much in *1984* when he anticipated that a continuous war would be needed to maintain his futuristic economy. To stop the Vietnam War we needed only to start paying for it. Had the American people been asked to finance the war by lowering their standard of living and paying higher taxes, it probably would have been brought to a swift conclusion. As it was, we borrowed billions from future generations and eventually debased the currency to repay it.

But you need not analyze national politics or foreign policy to see economics at work. Look at virtually any human endeavor and ask one simple question. Who will profit from this activity? Or in other words, follow the money. Ideally everyone will be making money. If General Motors builds a plant in Tennessee the company borrows money to finance it, thus putting someone's savings to work. Constructing the plant will create jobs, as will its operation. When the cars are sold, the proceeds go to the workers, the component suppliers, the bond holders and finally the stockholders in the form of dividends. The cars and trucks themselves add to the economy by making people more productive. When the trucks wear out, the steel is recycled for another product. While the process seems almost ideal, it is also very fragile. Vast amounts of capital and the lives of many individuals depend upon the success of the endeavor. When financial or economic uncertainty inhibits the risking of the capital, the plant does not get built and recession results. Jobs are not created, and unemployment rises. Since the capital is not invested, interest rates fall. The productivity of the nation declines and a vicious downward cycle begins. At this point the government may step in to reverse the downward cycle. There are many ways it can do this. By building a dam for example, it puts money in the hands of people who will in turn buy cars, thus creating more jobs at the car factory.

The point of this example is that our children can learn about economics by analyzing the events that surround their lives. Over a period of time they will develop a sixth sense that will add to their understanding and appreciation of the world they live in. This process of analysis can take the form of a continuous discussion between you and your child. At times you may know little more than the child; but by asking the obvious questions, a lively discussion will often result.

There are many subjects that will almost spontaneously provoke comment when brought up for discussion, for example, the role of government in the economy.

There is little debate within Western society that the democratic form of government is superior to any known alternative. The democracies are easily the richest, strongest, and most sophisticated countries on earth. Indeed, the backward state of much of the Third World is due primarily to those countries' lack of political sophistication. Democracies are characterized by a diffusion of political power mirrored by a diffusion of economic power. This latter part of the equation, the diffusion of economic power, is the focus of political debate in the Western world. Simple logic argues for centralization of economic power to coordinate effort and maximize efficiency. This central national planning is epitomized by the Japanese who have awed the world with their economic progress. But the counterargument is that centralization will corrupt the government and lead to bureaucratic inefficiencies. The Soviet Union's inability to feed itself is believed to be caused by its inefficient farm system and lack of decentralized control.

Which is right? Nobody knows; that is what the debate is all about. In America the pendulum of opinion swings back and forth. If the prevailing system satisfies the majority, it normally remains in place. If not, the pendulum may swing and the system will change to an alternative mode. For example, when the economy collapsed in the 1930's, the government stepped into a number of industries, regulating rates and establishing standards. In the 1970's, when the economy began to stagnate, this same government regulation was given part of the blame. One of the cornerstones to Ronald Reagan's economic policy was, therefore, deregulation or the decentralization of economic control. These swings of government involvement are always a matter of degree. Often they involve little more than the vigorous enforcement of existing laws. In an America that advocates personal freedom, the idea of government control is viewed by some as fundamentally undesirable. As a result, calls for government action are usually in response to an obvious wrong. Diane Sawyer details a polluted river on "Sixty Minutes" and pretty soon others begin to notice that their rivers are also polluted and join the crowd agitating for stricter pollution laws. While everyone is for clean rivers, not everyone is for the laws that will clean them up. For a business that is not polluting, the regulations become an unnecessary and costly burden, hence the opposition.

At times the debates can be frustrating but they do reflect democracy at work. Thoughtful Americans should always try to reach the substance of any national issue and separate the rhetoric from the reason. At the rhetoric level there is often much discussion of the benefits of free enterprise and the evils of socialism. The champions of each side will rally on the high ground of moral righteousness and claim that justice and compassion support their cause.

At a more pragmatic level, Americans usually will allocate authority to the party best able to get a particular job done. And when the job is done, that authority is sometimes withdrawn. The electorate, however, is not always as clever as this description may sound, because events often dictate the situation and are beyond the control of society. Franklin Roosevelt neither caused nor ended the Depression. He did ride the crest of that event and guide the American people by providing hope and confidence. This was the genius of his leadership; not the active but ineffective economics he implemented. The economic agenda of each decade is usually quite clear and the government will focus its rhetoric on the problem until it runs its natural course.

DEFICITS AND GOVERNMENT SPENDING

At the moment the major economic problem facing the nation is the deficit. Nothing much is being done about it, but it will probably go away over the next twenty years for some very simple reasons. The American population is aging. By the year 2000, 75 million Americans will be over fifty-five years of age. These rich and aging baby boomers will be buying less and will generate huge pools of savings that will offset the deficits their earlier demands created. America will swing from huge deficits to huge surpluses. As this trend manifests itself, the problem will cease to be publicly discussed. The Great Depression ended with the opening salvos of World War II just as the crash of 1929 signalled the end of prosperity in the twenties. While these great events can be analyzed and even predicted, they cannot always be controlled.

Government involvement in the economy is not a new idea. History is replete with examples of rulers tinkering with their economies. From the Pharaoh's pyramids to Nasser's Aswan High Dam, governments have instigated projects to create jobs and secure the wealth and health of the nation.

In modern times this tinkering codified into an economic theory sometimes called Keynesism. John Maynard Keynes, an Englishman who lived from 1883 to 1945, advocated that the government should borrow money and spend it when the private sector was either unable or afraid to. This spending by the government would create jobs, stimulate the economy and get things going again. He also advocated that when good times returned, government borrowings should be paid off. The American Congress liked the first part of Mr. Keynes' theory and has proven very adept at borrowing money and spending it on things like dams, rocketships and government jobs. However, they have had a problem getting the knack of the second part, which is to pay back what has been borrowed. As a result our national debt has increased. Right now the government spends about 23% of our gross national product, and our debt has been increasing right along with our spending. Richard Nixon once said, "We are all Keynesians now," by which he meant that government spending has been accepted by all parties. The following numbers bear out his statement.

GOVERNMENT SPENDING AS % OF GNP

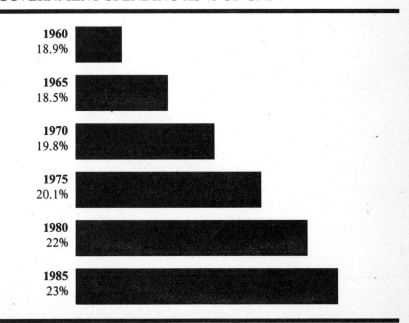

1960 18.9%	
1965 18.5%	
1970 19.8%	
1975 20.1%	
1980 22%	
1985 23%	

Source: Office of Management and Budget.

While the debate about who receives government spending is always vigorous, there is one part that is never debated. Bond holders around the world who have lent America money to build dams and rocketships, get paid every six months. As the pie chart shows, a vast amount of our budget (14%) is used just to pay debt.

WHERE IT GOES ...

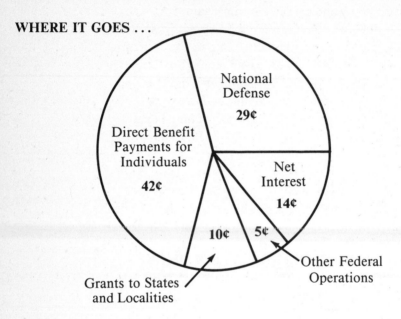

The major question each American has to answer is, are these numbers good or bad? Should we balance the budget and pay off the debt? If so, when or how quickly? What will happen if we do? Can we survive without rocketships and dams and government jobs? It is an important debate and how it is decided will affect most Americans. Obviously, if one is a builder of rocketships the effect could be severe, but even the most remote citizen will feel the pinch when the nation's biggest spender changes its habits.

USING ECONOMICS TO PROMOTE SOCIAL JUSTICE

The objective of our national economic policy must be to promote social justice. In concrete terms that means jobs, a reasonable standard of living, and stable prices. These objectives should achieve a certain freedom from want. Many believe that freedom from want is fundamental to citizenship, like freedom of speech and freedom of religion. Perhaps so, but it is certainly easier said than done. And it does give the government a mandate to guide the economy in any way it can. One major way of guiding the economy is by controlling money.

Today we take government control of money for granted. The idea that anybody else could create or print money is almost ludicrous. But, in fact, during the early years of the republic individual banks did issue money, which was used as legal tender in exchange for goods and to conduct business deals.

We might recall at this point just what banks do. Without being too cynical about it, banking is a shell game based on probability. Banks borrow money through one door and lend it out another. The difference between what they pay for borrowing and receive for lending is their profit. The probability aspect is based on the hope that their depositors, the ones they borrow from, will not all ask for their money at the same time. If they do, and the bank has lent some of its deposits as it is supposed to, it may not be able to meet the demand and might be forced to close its doors. This is, in fact, what happened with disturbing regularity in the nation's early days. The resulting fear, bankruptcy and unemployment cried out for a solution. Over the years the idea of a central bank to act as the depositor of last resort was debated. Finally, in 1913, the Congress created a central banking system, and named it the Federal Reserve System.

The Federal Reserve does not build roads, generate electricity, produce consumer goods or provide raw materials or labor. Nevertheless, it allows these physical parts of our economy to operate in a relatively stable financial environment. In the old days Christmas tree lights were strung in series. If one went out, they all went out. Later the bulbs were placed in parallel lines, so if one bulb went out the others still glowed. Similarly, the Federal Reserve prevents isolated bank failures from rippling through the economy and causing financial panic. The Federal Reserve can arrange for a failing bank to close its doors in an orderly fashion or simply lend it the money it needs to continue operating and get back on its feet.

MONETARISM

So important is the banking and money business that some people believe its control and manipulation are the most important determinants of economic performance. These people believe that proper control of the money supply can regulate the growth of the economy, restrain inflation and secure jobs. This theory has been labeled *monetarism*. One of its foremost advocates is Milton Friedman, who was awarded a Nobel Prize for his work in the field.

Essentially, monetarists advocate that money growth, properly controlled by the central bank, will achieve most of our economic objectives. Perhaps the foremost problem with this theory is the definition of money. We would all agree that the cash in our pockets is money. Our checking account down at the local bank, out of which we pay our bills, also can be construed as money, even though no printed cash represents it. How about our savings account and money market funds? You will have to ask your local monetarist. The point is that defining and measuring money is difficult and a core problem in practicing monetarism.

According to the theory, after defining and measuring money, the next problem is to control the supply. Either too much or too little money in the system will cause problems. Since our economy is growing, the supply of money must grow with it. The trick seems to be how much. If the money supply grows too quickly the theory says that it will cause inflation. For example, if five thirsty men, each with a nickel, are in a room with one glass of water, you would expect the price of that water to be five cents. But if you gave each man a dollar, the price would rise to a dollar, even though the supply and demand for the water has not changed. This phenomenon is known as inflation—an increase in prices due to an increase in the supply of money. To be sure, prices can rise and fall for other reasons, primarily because of changes in supply or demand for basic goods. But these price changes are healthy ones. For example, if people believe that eating oranges is beneficial to their health, their demand will increase the price of oranges. Farmers will use these profits to plant more oranges, until the supply of oranges equals the demand and prices stabilize.

The opposite of inflation is deflation, which the monetarists blame on a contraction of the money supply. If prices fall, production declines, unemployment increases and recession or depression results. The monetarists blame the depression of the 1930s on a severe contraction of the money supply. There was a so-called dollar shortage that caused prices to fall and production to decline. A lack of money, often referred to as a lack of liquidity, also affects the banking system and causes failure.

A recent example of the application of monetary theory took place in America in 1980. Coincidental with Ronald Reagan's election, the Federal Reserve began contracting the money supply. As a result, many basic commodity prices began to fall, for example, oil, minerals, and foodstuffs. Not surprisingly, oil wells, mines and farms began shutting down all over the country. Unemployment in these areas skyrocketed and bank failures became common. Tax cuts, creating huge federal deficits, stimulated the economy elsewhere and kept the entire country from falling into a similar state.

The monetarist argument is a strong one, but applying this theory in the real world is difficult and risky. Nevertheless, all Americans should realize that the theory exists and from time to time is the basis for economic decisions that affect all of our lives.

There is an important point to be made regarding the application of monetary theory. It is very common to say that the government prints money to pay it bills and that is what causes inflation. Of course, it is true that our money is printed in Washington at the Bureau of Engraving and Printing, which is part of the Treasury Department. But cash, or the paper and coin we carry in our pockets to do business with, is only a small part of what we call money. As mentioned before, checking and savings accounts, money market funds, and certificates of deposit are also considered money and represent the major portion of the money supply. It is the manipulation of these other parts that allows the government (Federal Reserve) to control the supply of money.

The Federal Reserve controls the supply of money in the economy by controlling the amount of money banks have to lend. For every dollar that a bank has on deposit, it is able to make loans equal to a percentage of those deposits. That critical percentage is dictated by the Federal Reserve and is called the reserve requirement. By increasing the reserve requirement, the amount of money available for loans is lowered.

There are two other ways the Federal Reserve uses the banking system to control the supply of money. One is the interest rate it charges banks to borrow money. Banks get money from a number of sources, the main one being customer deposits. But they are also allowed to borrow money from the Federal Reserve. By raising the rate at which they lend money, the Federal Reserve discourages borrowing and thereby lowers the money available for loans.

The other control is somewhat less direct. The Federal Reserve will from time to time buy or sell U.S. Treasury securities. If it buys securities, it puts money into the banking system, and that money is then available for loans. If it does the opposite, that is, sells securities, it will take money out of the system, thus lowering the money available for loans. These procedures are known as the open market operations of the Federal Reserve. So, while the term printing money is illustrative and often used, one should be aware of the actual methods that our central bank, the Federal Reserve, uses to create money, and the role commercial banks play in the process.

ECONOMIC DATA

Economics is normally considered a science, and like all scientific endeavors it requires measurement to test and confirm theoretical assumptions. The numbers and data associated with economic analysis are immense and subject to continuous debate. As already discussed, we measure the amount of money in our system. We also measure the number of people who are employed and the number who are not, the amount of goods we produce and the amount we sell to other countries. We measure the amounts the government, consumers and corporations spend. Economists discuss these measurements and speculate on their cause-and-effect relationships and what they mean to society.

The importance of the numbers depends on what is happening in the economy. During a recession the unemployment figure is watched very closely. If interest rates are high, the focus will shift to the money supply and inflation index. The glossary has easy definitions of these often quoted measurements. Probably the most common is the *gross national product* (GNP). Basically, the GNP measures the consumption of goods and services by the nation. It is usually broken down into the consumer (64 percent), business (16 percent), government (28 percent) and exports (−8 percent). Each of these sectors is broken down in turn into many subgroups. The importance of the GNP is not so much its size as its direction. If it declines, it signals a contracting economy, which implies serious social and political consequences. A declining

GNP will result in higher unemployment, a lower standard of living and eventually social discord. Nor does this decline have to be deep or prolonged for its effects to be felt. Our last recession was in 1981 and 1982. A recession is defined as two consecutive quarters of negative GNP. In the winter of 1981-2 the economy declined 4.5 percent in the fourth quarter of 1981 and 4.5 percent in the first quarter of 1982. These declines triggered unemployment increases of one percent or about one million jobs.

Ideally we would not have recessions, but it is the nature of our economy to move through cycles. That is, there are periods of expansion and periods of contraction. Through their analysis economists attempt to minimize these fluctuations, thereby promoting political stability. This cycle, sometimes called the business cycle, is a natural phenomenon that has repeated itself over the years.

As you would guess, no two recessions are alike. Decreased activity by the consumer or business sometimes can be offset by exports and government spending, but other times it cannot. Recently high interest rates have put a damper on economic activity, but we have also had recession in periods of low interest rates. This economic fluctuation requires constant attention, and to be aware of its effect on our lives is a responsibility of citizenship.

As mentioned, one of the parts of our GNP is the difference between what we import and export. If we export more than we import, our level of national wealth rises. The problem, however, is that our wealth may be someone else's poverty. If one nation accumulates wealth at the expense of its trading partners, political instability results. In an ideal world all nations would either be self-sufficient or have a balance between what they import and export. For example, Americans could grow wheat, the Italians make shoes, the Germans clocks, the British clothes and the Japanese TV sets. These various products could be traded around so every nation would have food, clothes, shoes, clocks, and TVs. But it does not work out that way. In a competitive world the Germans will learn how to make TVs. Not only do they stop buying TVs from Japan, they start selling them to the Italians. Meanwhile the Japanese have built TVs nobody wants and therefore have no money to buy wheat from the Americans or clothes from the British. What can the Japanese do? Well, for one thing, they can stop buying clocks from the Germans and use that money to buy wheat and clothes. Not a very satisfactory solution because they need clocks. Another thing they can do is print more money and see if the Americans and British will take it in exchange for clothes and food. All these machinations do in fact take place among nations on a continuous basis. The Japanese will raise barriers to stop the import of goods, and the British will deflate their currency to adjust their trade balance.

A good example of all this was the so called oil shocks of 1973 and 1978. The world's major producers of oil decided to raise the price of oil. They formed a cartel called OPEC (Organization of Petroleum Exporting Countries) and set higher prices on the oil they sold. Their purpose was to get richer. The United States, to pay for the oil, printed a lot of paper and gave it to the Arabs. The Arabs bought a lot of things with the paper including American bonds which went down in value. So the Americans, in a sense, gave with one hand and took away with the other. To be sure the Arabs are probably richer than before, but things did not work out exactly as they had planned. The printing of lots of dollars had some negative side effects like inflation, but did to some degree, take the political sting out of the OPEC price hike.

I hope this explanation will take the sting out of some of your child's questions! At the very least you should now have some real examples of how the economy affects all of us—in little ways and big ways.

Part I

Family Income

As children develop, they become keenly aware of their social position relative to their peers: a position determined by sex, ethnic origin, intelligence, physical attributes, and family status. Unlike some European societies, where family status may be determined by blood, an American family's status will be determined more often by wealth. The egalitarian nature of our democracy has fostered this system and its effect on the child is profound. Much of a child's self-esteem and confidence will result from this view of himself relative to his peers. If he is different, anxieties may arise that need to be understood and relieved. Ideally, a child's upbringing should not be affected by his family's income; but, in fact, much of his education is determined and influenced by his relative wealth or poverty.

Schools foster equality by stressing academic merit. The influence of wealth is diluted through the use of dress codes and other restrictions on material goods. Students are taught to judge an individual on his character not his income. The problems arise when the child observes the commercial world where all the awards seem to accrue to the person of wealth. The poor, regardless of their character, receive little. This dichotomy should be addressed by parents in the course of raising their children.

How does one do that? Simply by telling them the truth.

1

Where It Comes From

"Dad, how come Jimmy has a new car and we don't?"

TV AND REALITY

In the sixties, when the unraveling of the American nuclear family unit was getting under way, much was made of the unrealistic situations portrayed on television during our childhood. "The Ozzie and Harriet Show" was a favorite example for social commentators. The most vulnerable facet of the show was Ozzie's apparent lack of a job; he never worked. Every show seemed to start on Saturday morning. Ozzie never got fired or promoted or changed jobs. Some undiscussed and unidentified stream of cash kept the Nelson family properly clothed and sheltered. The normal tension associated with the family's income and standard of living was neatly written out of the script. The criticism was probably justified. No portrayal of American life is complete without a description of the economic forces that surround it. By contrast, in a recent episode of the "Bill Cosby Show" Vanessa was chided by her classmates for being rich after she tried to impress her friends by telling them the cost of a prized family painting. Dr. Huxtable and his lawyer wife patiently explained to Vanessa how hard they had worked to pay for the painting and other luxuries associated with their family's life. Of course, the hard work of a doctor and a lawyer pays a lot better than the hard work of a teacher or construction worker; but the episode pointed up the trouble children have understanding their place in our economic system.

A child needs to be aware of his family's relative level of income and the sources from which it is derived. Naturally the depth of this knowledge will depend on age and maturity. But as children become aware of the inequities that result from different levels of income, they should have the knowledge to place those inequities in perspective. Further, they should have some feeling for where they stand relative to peers and more importantly why. The purpose of educating children in this manner is to foster healthy attitudes towards wealth and income. If a child can view money and wealth objectively, much of the emotion and anxiety associated with the accumulation of material goods can be eliminated.

TELLING YOUR CHILDREN THE TRUTH

The question always arises as to how much and when a child should learn about the family's finances. Again, as in other areas of life, common sense should prevail. If a child asks a question, he should be given a straightforward, truthful answer couched in terms appropriate for his age. Keep in mind that the tendency towards secrecy is natural and should not be totally forgotten. If your nine-year-old asks you how much money you make, the answer need not be an exact number like $30,000. The child's question may just be curiosity stemming from some school experience. Conversation among playmates often deals with family income or material acquisitions like cars or homes. One of the great benefits of neighborhoods and neighborhood schools is the assumption of similar income levels. I say assumption because appearances can be deceiving. But to the child appearances are everything and similarity fosters contentment, while difference can foster anxiety.

So if your nine-year-old asks about the family's income, use the question as an opening to a general discussion of money. The easiest way might be to back into the answer by evaluating the costs of the family home, cars, food, and so forth. This process may not result in a number approximating your income but it will probably satisfy him and be instructional in the process. If he is genuinely curious he must be given truthful answers, at least enough to satisfy his curiosity. If his curiosity is superficial he will probably lose interest in your game and the subject will pass.

Also parents need to guard against information being abused by children who might use it to brag to classmates, the "my daddy makes more money than yours" type of thing. But more important, money is an abstraction to most children, and a direct answer would be meaningless. To tell a nine-year-old that you make $30,000 a year is to tell him nothing.

Questions from older children should be dealt with as frankly as possible. Eventually your child will have to arrange the finances of his own life. If he is going to be either helped or hindered by your family's finances, he should understand why, for example, what kind of education are you able and willing to support. And if your child will need to work, he should be prepared for it.

LEVELS OF INCOME

Families should try to adapt their lifestyles to their level of income. To live otherwise often effects the family's happiness and the self-esteem of its members. If parents can understand and accept the consequences of their income, the children will also. The senseless anxiety generated by the belief that there is a correlation between additional wealth and happiness will be eliminated. It would be spurious to say that abject poverty is not a source of unhappiness; it definitely is. But it is equally false to believe that a Mercedes Benz owner should be measurably happier than the owner of a Chevrolet.

The distribution of income in the United States is not random in the sense that the level of one's income is a matter of chance. But neither can it be precisely determined in advance. To the extent that it is random, or left to chance, some statistical evidence can be useful. We know for example that on average, Harvard graduates will make more money than noncollege graduates. But we also know that a few people who do not graduate from college will make more money than many Harvard graduates.

As the following table indicates, about 60 percent of householders in the United States over the age of twenty-five have incomes between $20,000 to $75,000 per year.

	25 to 34	35 to 44	45 to 54	55 to 64	65 to 74
$20,000 to $29,000	23.3	20.2	17.2	18.0	17.0
$30,000 to $39,999	17.8	18.7	16.3	13.5	8.8
$40,000 to $49,999	10.1	12.6	13.1	10.1	4.5
$50,000 to $59,999	5.2	8.6	9.6	6.8	2.5
$60,000 to $74,999	3.4	6.3	7.8	5.5	1.8
Other	40.1	33.7	35.9	46.1	65.3
All households	100.0%	100.0%	100.0%	100.0%	100.0%
Median income	$25,100	$31,100	$33,200	$35,600	$15,400

Source: Reprinted with permission, Copyright *American Demographics* 1987.

FACTORS AFFECTING INCOME

Not surprisingly, one of the factors affecting income is age. If a ten-year-old child's father is thirty-years-old, it is likely his family has less income than one whose father is forty. The two ten-year-olds are in the same grade and are equally intelligent, but one of them has a computer, goes on ski trips and always has the best sports equipment. For a ten-year-old boy to have a relatively young father may be an adequate trade-off for the lower income; nevertheless the financial difference is real and visible.

Another factor affecting family income is marital status. Married couples have higher levels of income than single-parent families. In most cases divorce results in a lower standard of living. With all the other traumas associated with divorce, the subtle effect of a lower standard of living should not be ignored. Animosity and resentment toward a parent can hinge on something as simple as a lost trip to summer camp. If there is one lesson a child might learn from his parent's divorce it could be that financially divorce is very inefficient. Or more simply if you want to enhance your standard of living try to stay married.

Another major influence on family income is education. As the following table indicates, the higher the level of education the higher the family's income.

This fact will come as no surprise to adults, but children, depending on their personal circumstances, may not be as quick to pick up on it. If

Where It Comes From

Household Income	Percentage of Household headed by a College Graduate
Under $10,000	5.9%
$10,000 - 14,999	6.0
$15,000 - 19,999	7.8
$20,000 - 24,999	8.6
$25,000 - 34,999	18.0
$35,000 - 49,999	22.5
$50,000 - 74,999	19.5
$75,000 and over	11.7

Source: Reprinted with permission, Copyright *American Demographics* 1987.

a child lives in a parochial environment where most parents are well educated, like a college campus, he may take education as a given and attribute differences in income to other factors. Likewise children raised in an environment where most parents do not attend college may also conclude that education is not a major determinant of income. In both cases, this would be a grievous misconception. In middle class America there is a consistent statistical correlation between levels of education and income.

The effect of health on a family's level of income is also significant. A family that sustains a personal health crisis will probably sustain a similar crisis in income. Whether it be the burden of an impoverished and ill grandparent, an alcoholic parent, or a child requiring special medical treatment, the family's standard of living and income will be diminished.

Statistics therefore, take some of the mystery out of personal incomes. If you meet an American and can ascertain a few facts about his age, education, family's health, place of residence, and occupation, you can bracket his income fairly closely. It should also be pointed out that most Americans work for a living. Only about 23 percent of incomes are received from other sources, those being primarily investments and Social Security.

WHAT MAKES THE DIFFERENCE

Income is only half the story when talking about American living standards. I once had for clients two women named Barbara and Jennifer. They were both married and each lived on an income of more than

$60,000 a year. In each case about $15,000 came from family trusts and the remainder from their own and their husbands' salaries. Their lifestyles, however, were somewhat different.

Barbara's monthly income

Income:

Salary	$3,750	
Trust income	1,250	
Rental property income	750	
Total	$5,750 × 12 = $69,000 Annual Income	

Expenses:

House payments	1,600
Car payments	800
Resort home payments	700
Taxes	650
Savings	—
Other	2,000
Total	$5,750

Jennifer's monthly income

Income:

Salary	$3,750	
Trust income	1,250	
Total	$5,000 × 12 = $60,000 Annual Income	

Expenses:

House payments	$1,250
Car payments	300
Taxes	800
Savings	650
Other	2,000
Total	$5,000

Barbara's family owned a larger home in a more prestigious neighborhood, a resort condominium, and two foreign cars. Jennifer's family, on the other hand, owned a smaller home, two domestic cars and no investment properties. The apparent difference in standard of living and net worth was caused by two fundamental factors about which every family must decide. The first is how the family allocates its income or more simply, what it spends it on. The second is how much the family borrows to extend that income. Let's see how Barbara and Jennifer allocated their monthly income to achieve their lifestyles.

Barbara's family was able to afford a larger home and more expensive cars by not saving any of their income. Furthermore, they borrowed as much as the banks would allow them given their level of income. Their resort condominium paid for itself and provided a tax shelter, so less of their income went to pay taxes. Barbara also made some profit on her earlier homes and put all of it into her current home. Jennifer, on the other hand tended to save more and as a result lived more modestly and paid more taxes.

To some there is no question that Barbara is the shrewder money manager; she has gotten more than Jennifer out of the same resources. Perhaps, but there were different attitudes and circumstances that prompted the different strategies. First, Barbara was younger than Jennifer and felt more comfortable taking on risk in the form of debt. Second, she believed that her condominium would always be worth at least what she paid for it, and that the rent would cover her monthly payment to the bank. In addition, she believed that saving was unnecessary because she expected to inherit enough money to live on in her old age, and that the equity in her real estate investments provided additional savings.

Jennifer was older than Barbara and felt less comfortable taking on debt. Her income as a salesperson was less reliable than her husband's job with the government; hence, she feared that high fixed monthly debt payments to pay for cars, credit cards, or vacations could threaten her lifestyle if her salary was interrupted for even a short period of time. Unlike Barbara, Jennifer feared that her inheritance could be eroded by an expensive terminal illness of one of her parents. In the end she might have to provide for herself. Therefore, she preferred to accumulate her savings in financial assets rather than building up equity in her home and other real estate holdings.

Which course will eventually prove to be the most successful only time will tell. In America risk-taking is often rewarded handsomely. But risk implies danger and loss. History books are replete with examples of financial disaster in virtually every generation and economic sector. Barbara's assumptions that her real estate will always be worth what she paid for it, and that her debt payments will always be manageable, may not prove correct. If she is not right, the financial burden could be severe.

INVESTMENT INCOME

Investments and investment income contribute significantly to the American standard of living. As pointed out below most family income is earned.

Income Source	% of Total
Earnings (wages, salaries, self-employment)	78.3%
Interest and dividends (including estates & trusts)	6.8
Social Security	6.7
Pensions (private and government)	4.0
Other	4.2
Total	100.0%

Source: Reprinted with permission, copyright *American Demographics* 1987.

Nevertheless investment income, like interest payments, stock dividends and rents generate billions of dollars of income annually. These income generating assets can be inherited, purchased with personal savings, or accumulated in a pension fund. A little investment income can supplement earned income and make a marginal difference in a family's standard of living. Only about 8 percent of American income comes from interest, dividends, rents and other forms of so-called unearned income. What is perhaps more important is that the number of families receiving interest from banks is almost equal to the number of families with earned income. This means that most families, to one degree or another, derive some portion of their income from savings.

Sometimes parents have a hard time finding reasons why saving is important. Independence from labor is a good one to remember. The more traditional reasons are to save for a rainy day, meaning provision for some unforeseen family disaster that may mean the end of a regular income, or for a major expense like college education. However, income from savings is a measurable aspect of family income and can make a difference in the family's standard of living.

This is an important concept for children to understand. Savings are not simply money lying fallow in some bank vault. Savings are assets which provide income to enhance your lifestyle. More importantly, no work is required to earn this income, only the passage of time. And yes there are many people whose income from savings is such that they do not have to work at all.

The way it is usually expressed is something like this, "She has a little money on the side" or "His family has money," which means that he receives income from a pool of savings created by a successful ancestor. These pools of savings are often in the form of trusts. A trust is simply an agreement whereby a third party, like a lawyer or a bank, will temporarily be given some asset, often cash, by one individual, to hold for the benefit of another.

The reasons parents and grandparents set up trusts rather than give the money directly to a child are the obvious ones. If the child is a minor and cannot manage the money, the trust is the agreement whereby an individual or bank will take care of it temporarily until the child can handle his own affairs. Another reason is to arrange for professional investment advice so that the assets are not lost through financial mismanagement.

There are also tax advantages which sometimes will prompt establishment of a trust. For example, the most common form of a trust may be the Uniform Gift to Minor Account. The law in most states allows parents to establish an account for their child whereby the parent is the custodian (meaning trustee) and the child is the beneficiary. Prior to the 1986 Tax Reform Act the income from such an account belonged to the child and was taxed to the child. Presumably the child paid fewer taxes than the parent and, hence the account (trust) acted as a tax shelter. If the parent intended for the savings to go for the child's future education, there seemed little harm in giving the money to the child a little early, if it would save some taxes. The Tax Reform Act of 1986 has changed the rules a bit. The income from such an account is now taxed to the parent until the child reaches age 14.

WHEN YOUR CHILD HAS THE LARGER INCOME

Another family problem that might threaten an adult child's future is financing a parent's retirement. Parents can become impoverished through ill health, bad business decisions, or simply bad luck. Adult children can quickly find themselves responsible for the care and housing of a parent. The sooner they are aware of these problems the better.

I once had a widowed client aged fifty-eight who had an annual income of $27,000 a year based on Social Security and a portfolio of securities, valued at $375,000. Her husband had been a successful small businessman and the family had always lived very comfortably. Unfortunately, at age fifty-five the father had borrowed a substantial amount of money to expand his business and a year later suffered a fatal heart attack. Their two daughters were both married and comfortably raising their own families. When the family business was sold, the debts paid, and the estate probated, my client settled into retirement based on the assets described above. Like many women of her generation, my client had not been involved in the family's financial matters other than to manage a budget for food, clothing and utilities. She had a small savings account of her own, but the bulk of the family's assets were in the business, with which she had very little to do. The cash from the estate was given to my bank to manage on the advice of the family attorney.

Her retirement lifestyle would no longer be financed by her husband's roofing business, but rather by an impersonal bank, managing a portfolio of financial securities which she understood not one wit. For reasons that are fairly common in her generation, my client insisted that any income derived from her securities be paid out to her immediately. Since stocks and bonds pay dividends and interest at different times, the income flow was erratic in both frequency and amount. Unable to budget this cash flow, my client began to spend more than she was earning and eventually began to erode her portfolio's principal. In other words she was slowly strangling the goose that laid her golden egg. Given her age, I could see that her rate of spending would eventually leave her destitute and undoubtedly dependent on her two children.

For reasons of confidentiality a trust officer cannot always act to prevent a perceived disaster. In this case, although I warned my client repeatedly, she continued to live beyond her means, including making gifts to her children that she could ill afford. Finally, one of her daughters asked me whether her mother was wise to make such generous gifts. I seized the opportunity to suggest a family meeting. Even though the mother had refused my suggestions for such a meeting, she readily acquiesced to her daughters and we were finally able to get all the cards on the table.

Once the circumstances were made clear, there was an audible easing of tension. A budget was established and I was authorized to make fixed monthly remittances similar to the household allowance she received during her marriage. The daughters were allowed access to my reports so they could monitor their mother's financial status. In addition to these money matters, we arranged for the daughters to have their mother's power of attorney in case she became ill and unable to act for herself. Finally she agreed to have her will rewritten to smooth out the settlement of her estate when that occurred. None of these matters was profound but, had they not been resolved the disruption in the daughters' families could have been severe. An earlier resolution of the problem had been blocked by the inability of the mother and daughters to talk about money in an objective and open manner.

ACTIVITIES

1. Use the natural occasions which arise in family conversations to discuss the sources and limits of your family income. Depending on your child's age you may want to avoid specifics. Nevertheless, a certain knowledge of what various jobs pay can facilitate the discussion. The U.S. Department of Labor Statistics publishes an annual *Occupational Outlook Handbook*, which gives descriptions and projections for several hundred occupations in major industries. This book is available from the Superintendent of Documents, U.S. Government Printing Office, Washington, D.C. 20402, and from regional offices of the Bureau of Labor Statistics. Your local library will have a copy. It is a very useful source of information about what jobs will be paying in the future to help your child understand how his career choice will affect his earning and spending power.

2

Where It Goes

"Mom, may I have ten dollars for the movies?"

Ever wonder where Americans spend their hard earned incomes? Take a look at the following chart for the answer:

1982-1984	1982-1984 (in percent)
Food and beverages	20.1
Housing	39.2
Apparel	6.5
Transportation	21.2
Medical care	3.9
Entertainment	4.1
Other goods and services	5.0
Total	100.0%

Source: Reprinted with permission, Copyright *American Demographics* 1987.

These numbers should come as no surprise to most Americans. Food, shelter, clothing, and transportation have always taken the biggest bite out of our budgets. By the time they leave the nest children should also be aware of these facts, not only because most of them will live by them for the greater portion of their lives, but also to put their current expenditures into perspective. Let me illustrate.

I once had a client who was the scion of a wealthy family in Philadelphia. His annual income from age twenty-one was in excess of $100,000 a year. He worked little and lived modestly, except for one extravagance. He spent vast amounts of money on formula "V" racing cars. The sport was his avocation and primary interest. When he married, his wife began making equally extravagant expenditures on clothes from the same income. Needless to say, a family crisis ensued. Eventually they reached an agreement on how much of the family's income was to be spent on cars, clothes and so forth. In a word, they had to budget.

When a family includes children, the need to budget becomes even more important. It is not necessarily because the family fears overspending that it should budget; your checkbook will tell you when you are out of cash. Rather, families should budget because there are limits to any level of income.

If your child asks if he can buy a $40 jacket, the question isn't really whether you can afford it. The question is whether you want to spend $40 on clothes or something else. Even the federal government, with a trillion dollars to spend, has to decide whether it wants another submarine or more money for schools, and the decision is never an easy one.

This concept of limits is important because it presents the child with the concept of making choices. Choosing leads to quantification, valuation and trading off. The big decisions of marriage, children, jobs and education will come later. The training ground for those decisions may well be at the local mall.

THE FAMILY HOME

For most families a large portion of their income will go to finance their home. A house represents more to American families than a place to come in from the rain. The neighborhood you live in can reflect not only your income, but your self-image. Furthermore, because of rising real estate prices, the family home increasingly represents a family's savings and net worth. A big part of the American dream is owning your own home. And the more expensive the home, the more the dream has come true, or so many of us think.

One day my eleven-year-old daughter Rebecca and I dropped off a classmate at her new home. Becky, whose sole objective in life is to be near her friends, suggested that we buy the house next door, which happened to be up for sale. It was much newer but about the same size as our present home. However, primarily because of location, it was valued at twice what the homes were in our old city neighborhood. The easy answer to Becky would have been to say that we could not afford it. While true, this answer would not have meant much given her limited knowledge of home financing. Instead, I asked her how much she thought the house cost. She of course had no idea. So we called the agent whose name appeared on the for sale sign and asked her. She told us $300,000. I then rhetorically asked Becky if she knew how such a home would be financed. Having received the obligatory "no," I explained that at least 20 percent of the value or $60,000 would be required in cash as a down payment. I further explained that many people get this money from the sale of their existing home or from savings. The remainder could then be borrowed from a bank. In this case you would need $240,000. Since banks lend money based on your ability to pay, you would need an income of about $100,000 per year. I then stated that our income was less than $100,000 a year and that is why we could not buy it. She seemed satisfied with that and the discussion ended.

I think Rebecca was mildly interested in what I said, but I think she appreciated most the time I took to explain the matter. As mundane as the subject was, it nevertheless allowed us to talk about something other than her behavior, a topic that so often dominates discussions between parents and children.

Since parents of curious children might be called upon to have the basics of home financing at their fingertips, here are a couple of worksheets to help you do just that. They can be worked backwards or forwards. You can determine how much house a given salary will buy or how much income someone would need to afford a given house.

The mortgage worksheet simply adjusts your monthly income to determine how much money the bank will lend you. After you determine what you can borrow, add to it what you can put down and, presto, you know how much house you can afford. The mortgage worksheet is filled out for a family with an annual income of $30,000 and a $115 monthly car payment.

Mortgage Payment

Gross monthly income ($30,000 ÷ 12)	$ 2,500
Less any long-term debt, such as car payment	− 115
Net monthly income	$ 2,385
Multiply by .28 for a 90% loan; .32 for 80%	× .32
Monthly payment you can afford	$ 763
Less taxes and insurance (calculate the annual amount, then divide by 12)	− 167
Maximum monthly mortgage payment you can afford	$ 596

Taking your maximum monthly payment, go to the following table and enter at the current mortgage interest rate (let's say 10 percent). You can afford a mortgage of about $67,000 or about 2.3 times your $30,000 annual income.

Monthly Payment You Can Afford	Current Interest Rate for Mortgage Loan			
	9%	10%	11%	12%
$ 300	$ 37,284	$ 34,185	$ 31,501	$ 29,165
400	49,712	45,580	42,002	38,887
500	62,140	56,975	52,502	48,608
600	74,568	68,370	63,003	58,330
700	86,995	79,765	73,503	68,052
800	99,423	91,160	84,004	77,773
900	111,851	102,555	94,504	87,495
1,000	124,279	113,950	105,005	97,217

Monthly Payment You Can Afford	Current Interest Rate for Mortgage Loan		
	13%	14%	15%
$ 300	$ 27,120	$ 25,319	$ 23,726
400	36,159	33,759	31,634
500	45,199	42,198	39,543
600	54,239	50,638	47,451
700	63,279	59,078	55,360
800	72,319	67,517	63,269
900	81,359	75,967	71,177
1,000	90,399	84,397	79,086

A quick calculation of cash available for a down payment indicates that you have an additional $5,600 to buy a house.

Total cash available	$8,000
Less closing costs (as a rough estimate on a new mortgage with about two points, figure 4% of the mortgage amount for closing costs)	−2,400
Cash available for down payment	$5,600

Total value of the house you can afford then is 5,600 + 67,000 = $72,600

If you can afford a larger monthly payment than those shown on our table use the mortgage factors below. Simply take the monthly payment you can afford and divide by the factor appropriate for the interest rate prevailing at the time.

Interest Rate	Factor
8%	.00735
9%	.00805
10%	.00878
11%	.009523
11.5%	.009903
12%	.010286
12.5%	.010673
13%	.011062

EXAMPLE:

Monthly Payment	Interest Rate	Factor	Potential Mortgage
$1,756	10%	.00878	$200,000

FAMILY INSURANCE

John LeCheminant, a chartered financial consultant in Cross Keys, Maryland, prides himself on being able to take the mystery out of insurance. I agree that he can and questioned him at length on how to approach the subject with children. As in most money matters the best time to offer an explanation is when the subject comes up in normal conversation. "Daddy what happens if that tree falls on our house?" "Mommy, what happens to the car if we have an accident?" The quick answer is, "We have insurance." If follow-up questions like "What is insurance?" are asked, here are some of John's answers.

When you buy insurance you replace the uncertainty of a catastrophic loss with the certainty of small regular loss, which is the insurance premium payment. For example, there is no way of knowing whether you will be in an automobile accident. If you do not buy automobile insurance, then you are willing to risk paying for repairs to your car if it is damaged. You may also incur significant claims against you for damage to other people and their property. So people choose the relatively small premium for the peace of mind it gives them.

In truth a family cannot function without insurance. A catastrophic monetary loss would be so ruinous to a family's finances that operating an automobile, for example, simply would be too risky. But automobile accidents are just one of the events we insure against.

PROPERTY AND CASUALTY INSURANCE   In addition to automobiles, we protect our homes, furniture, jewelry, and other possessions against loss from fire, theft, and other forms of destruction by purchasing property and casualty insurance. We also protect ourselves against potential lawsuits when people are injured on our property. This is generally known as liability insurance and it is a part of the property and casualty market. An excellent example of how completely insurance permeates our lives was the recent case involving the Columbia Recreation Association in Columbia, Maryland. At its indoor swimming pool, the association built a giant water slide. Pool members however were unable to use the slide because the Association could not find anyone who would insure them against claims from a child or adult who was injured going down the slide. Eventually they were able to purchase the required insurance, but the importance of insurance in the conduct of even the most routine matters of modern American life was made very clear. You can probably find similar examples in your own community.

LIFE INSURANCE   In explaining life insurance, John is fond of saying that there are only two sources of income, namely, people working for money or money working for people. If a wage earner dies, life insurance will create a pool of money which, if properly invested, will generate a stream of income to replace the lost wages. Even very wealthy people who already have large amounts of invested capital earning money, often will need life insurance to replace assets used to pay estate taxes. As estates get larger, settling the estate becomes more and more complex and more and more costly. So John recommends that people with estates of $1 million dollars or more do at least two things. The first is to plan their estate settlement so that the impact of taxes and settlement costs is minimized. Second, having done that, determine the need for liquidity in the estate and make sure that there is sufficient life insurance to provide that liquidity. For most of us life insurance has become a necessity because it guarantees our family's income especially for raising and educating our children. This makes us feel more secure, even if the premium payments lower our standard of living slightly by eating up cash that otherwise could be spent on something else.

Insurance salesman often emphasize that there is a savings or investment aspect to life insurance. This is true, but it is a secondary function. The purpose of insurance is first and foremost to provide for catastrophic loss. If you want to save money there are better ways to do it than buying life insurance policies.

Most people purchase auto, life and homeowner's insurance out of their income. Other forms of insurance like disability and health are often acquired through "Group Insurance" at one's place of employment. Some examples are:

DISABILITY INCOME   Another catastrophic loss that parents need to insure against, is the loss of the ability to work because of injury or sickness. Disability income insurance provides income if this occurs. Disability income is divided broadly into short-term disability which may pay benefits for only six months, and long-term disability, which either pays to age sixty-five or in some cases for the remainder of an individual's life.

MEDICAL INSURANCE   The final type of catastrophic loss that families need to insure against is medical expense. Almost everyone is familiar with the organizations known as Blue Cross and Blue Shield. These institutions along with commercial insurance companies, and in some cases the federal government through Medicare and Medicaid, provide the insurance that is required to take care of medical expenses. Again, a small periodic payment is made to preclude a catastrophic payment later on. If you remain healthy, all those premiums will never be recouped; but they will have bought some well earned peace of mind.

INSURANCE COMPANIES   Your child may ask, "How do insurance companies work?" The answer is that insurance, like banking, is built on probability. People, called underwriters, who issue insurance, must know the probability that a given event will occur. For example, suppose you wished to protect your income against disability. The underwriter must determine the probability of people your age, health and occupation being involved in a disabling injury or sickness. To do this he consults a morbidity table. Morbidity, mortality and other such tables of probability are calculated by actuaries. Actuaries are experts in the theory and practice of life and other forms of insurance. They calculate the odds that a given event will take place. Once the odds are known, a price for the insurance premium can be determined.

Suppose we wish to insure one hundred people at age thirty for $1,000 of life insurance for one year. Let us imagine we consult a mortality table which tells us the probability is three in one hundred that an individual will die within one year. If we insure one hundred people, the probable claims that the underwriter will have to pay would be three deaths times $1,000 or $3,000. If we divide this risk among the one hundred people, then the cost would be $30 per person. In actual fact, the probability and therefore the cost would be far lower than this, but these figures give you the general principles.

Like any financial service much of the mystery is in the jargon. Use the glossary at the back of the book, and ask questions whenever discussing the subject with a salesman.

CREDIT

In contemporary America virtually everyone will choose at one time or another to use credit to finance a purchase. For parents the message is clear, at a fairly early age children should begin to develop a facility for evaluating offers to borrow money. Whether it be revolving credit, a real estate loan or some deferred payment plan, consumers need to evaluate and analyze the true cost of their purchase.

Jim Johnson is President of Loyola Federal Savings and Loan in Baltimore. He has spent a lifetime lending people money. A thoughtful father who consciously raised his children to be self sufficient and appreciate the value of a dollar, he admits to a failure in his instruction.

"I wish I had taught them more about credit," he says. We discussed the subject and agreed that schools could aid their students immensely by teaching the basic principle of borrowing. Johnson believes that credit is a useful tool and should be used wisely. He fears that given the easy access to credit by virtually any consumer, if it is not used wisely, it will surely be used unwisely. Consumers may be able to judge the products they are buying but not be able to calculate their cost because they cannot calculate the true finance charges.

The consumer's unfamiliarity with the true cost of credit is such that cars are often sold based on the financing arrangement. "Five percent financing, 0 percent financing," shout the advertisements, even though the total cost of the car to the consumer has not changed a bit. Since borrowing is simply the opposite of lending (or investing), we can focus on cash to calculate the cost of our credit. As with investing, the jargon helps turn the mathematics into a mystery, but a few examples might help. The real mystery is the relationship between price and time. If a car dealer says he will give you 4.2 percent financing or $1,000 rebate, what is he really saying?

Car Price	3 Year Total Interest	Total Cost of Car	Monthly Payment
$16,500 financed at 4.2%	$1,090	$17,590	$488.62/mo
OR			
$15,500 financed at 8.4%	$2,090	$17,590	$488.62/mo

One way or another the car dealer (or bank if you finance with it) is going to get $18,711 out of you over the next three years and in return you are going to get a car. The monthly payment and interest calculations are not complex. You can purchase a book of interest tables in most bookstores which will compute the numbers a salesman will quote you. It is well worth the effort. Any credit purchase should be analyzed to determine the real cost of an item, and the real rate of interest.

The credit game in real estate is played a little differently and naturally has its own jargon. One of realtors' favorite words is *points*. Technically, a point is 1 percent of the mortgage, but as with the car loan it is just another way of adjusting the price.

For example: You contract to buy a house for $120,000 and agree to put $20,000 down and finance $100,000. The bank says okay; it will lend you $100,000 at 10 percent plus three points. This is another way of saying it will lend you $97,000 calculated on the basis of $100,000. This will raise the bank's return from 10 percent to something a little higher, like 10.36 percent, and increase your downpayment to $23,000. However, being the clever one that you are, you get the seller to pay one of the points, which means that instead of selling the house for $120,000 he is selling the house for $119,000.

Instead of saying that the house sold for $120,000 with $20,000 down and $100,000 financed at 10 percent plus three points (split between the buyer and seller), we could say that the house sold for $119,000 with a $22,000 downpayment, and $97,000 financed at 10.36 percent.

The bond markets adjust prices the same way. If you look in the *Wall Street Journal* you see that U.S. Treasury bonds and notes of similar maturities will have different interest coupons, say 7 3/8%, 9 5/8% and 11 3/4%. Which is the better bond to invest in? Well, the market, like the bank making a mortgage loan, will adjust the price of all the bonds to the yield it wants at any particular point in time.

For example:

Bond (two year approximate maturity)	Price of a $10,000 Bond	Yield to Maturity
11 3/4% U.S. Treasury	$10,700	7.2%
9 5/8% U.S. Treasury	$10,400	7.2%
7 3/8% U.S. Treasury	$10,000	7.2%

Which is the better bond to buy? It depends on what happens to interest rates. If they go up you want to own the 10 percent coupon; if they go down you want the 7 percent bond.

Bond calculations can become quite complex because of time factors involved with varying maturities. I have simplified my example for purposes of illustration. But again you can purchase tables or special calculators to do the work for you. The main thing is to recognize the existence of the relationship among price, rate of interest, and time.

ACTIVITIES

---

1. Prepare a family budget with your children. Tell your children how much you are willing to spend on their clothes or other items. Suggest trade-offs they can make to acquire the things

they want, such as using their savings or earning additional income by babysitting or household chores.

2. Let your children plan a vacation and calculate the expenses such as gas and motels. Then let them record the expenses during the course of the trip.

3. Go to a car dealership and look at the prices of cars. Calculate car payments per month for various models.

4. Take your child grocery shopping, give him a budget and a list of items to purchase. Take a calculator and make trade-offs as you shop.

5. Encourage your child's school to arrange for local business talent to teach students about credit. Bankers, brokers and real estate agents would be a good place to start. Then evaluate various advertisements for auto sales and real estate to develop a hands-on facility for evaluating credit proposals.

6. Consider loaning your child money for some purchase. Then monitor the payback closely. This exercise is especially useful when the child is still paying for something he has shelved and no longer wants.

3

Where the Kids Come In

"But, Dad, I've already spent my allowance!"

KIDS AND CASH

John Peterman heads the Middle School at McDonogh School in Maryland. When asked about kids and the cash they receive, his answer is straightforward and simple: "It's too much." Like all of us he is aware of the importance of money in America's capitalistic culture. The benefits of our wealth surround us. But there is also a corrupting aspect to money and it manifests itself most often with cash. Peterman believes many children receive a cash allowance, which can be spent pretty much as they please. To a child, money given under such conditions may be viewed as a source of amusement. Cash, however, is very indiscriminate. It can be used to buy drugs as well as candy. It can be spent on computer software or given away in a vain attempt to buy friendship. It can be accumulated to purchase a much desired piece of clothing or squandered on junk.

The negative aspects of cash manifest themselves most often when there are no strings attached. Nevertheless, many parents rightly believe that children need to get involved in handling money. Fairly early

29

in their development children begin to ask for money to make purchases of their own choosing. Whether children want money for candy, comic books or baseball cards, many parents begin handing it out, knowing that it will be used for fairly specific purposes. The problems arise when the money and its eventual use are not controlled by the parent. The amount of money is not as important as is its final distribution.

The purpose of an allowance should be to transfer the responsibility for some cash purchases from the parent to the child. This responsibility should increase with age and, it is hoped, prepare the child for handling his own finances later on. It is important to remember that when a child receives cash, he has to decide immediately whether or not to spend it for the purpose for which it was intended. Just because a child is given lunch money does not mean that he has no choice on how to spend it. Many of my high school classmates financed their cigarette habits by eating less than well rounded lunches.

Some examples of cash purchases that could be transferred to the child at various ages and funded by an allowance include:

Age	Purpose
9	Candy
11	School supplies
13	Party gifts
15	Clothes
17	Gasoline, car insurance

Of course, children do get money from other sources. Gifts from relatives on special occasions are one. Even though parents do not provide this cash personally, they still should designate its use. A good rule of thumb is to allow the child to spend it on something approved by the parent or to save it. To allow them to stick excess cash in their pocket is to suggest that it can be spent on impulse, a very poor habit to encourage. A child should be taught that money is a scarce resource, that every dime should be saved or spent prudently. This advice is as true for Paul Mellon as it is for the most impoverished ghetto youth.

However, Marian Randall, a family counselor, cautions against excess supervision. "A child must have the right to fail," she says. Unless a child can make mistakes and experience the consequences, no benefit will be gained by the cash-handling experience. An allowance encumbered by too many strings will cause resentments and trigger rebellion rather than responsibility. Obviously there are trade-offs here which each parent much decide.

What about money earned outside the home and family? Certainly there is a tendency to say, "She earned it, she can keep it." It is a nice thought but sometimes it is premature. Some children are unquestionably very responsible with the money they earn. They invest in savings accounts or use it to purchase worthwhile and necessary items. In fact, most children who are responsible enough to hold a job are responsible enough to handle their salary. Still some are not, and even the responsible ones can use a little guidance.

The easiest way to influence a child's spending is to limit your own expenditures for their needs. If a daughter earns $50 a week on part-time jobs, ask her to assume responsibility for a portion of her clothes budget, or perhaps pay for her school lunch if that involves a daily cash outlay. Her response might be, "That's not fair. If I weren't working you would give me that money." This of course is true. In response you might agree to continue funding her lunches and wardrobe, if she promises to save her salary for future purchases. The situation to avoid is the excess cash burning a hole in the child's pocket, thereby creating impulse-buying habits.

Without getting too puritanical about it, impulse spending like compulsive consumption in general should be viewed as a less than desirable personal trait.

I once had a client who was the beneficiary of several trusts, which produced about $300,000 annually. Despite this rather handsome income he constantly spent $30,000 a year more than his trusts earned. He did this by simply asking the trustees to distribute a portion of the income-producing assets. Under the terms of the trust, the trustee, my bank, was authorized to do this. Unfortunately, each time the trust distributed some of the assets, the income-produced by the trust naturally declined. We adjusted the assets by buying higher income-producing securities in an effort to maintain income. Nevertheless, it was a period of declining interest rates, and eventually the distributions from the trust took their toll. His income declined each year, right along with his standard of living.

The problem was his consumption. Like the overweight person who consumes more calories than his body needs to sustain itself, the compulsive consumer has developed a pleasure bond with the material consumption of goods. He will spend without purpose or limit. I believe these habits often are developed during childhood to compensate for other emotional deficiencies, or from simply having excess money to spend, without parental guidance or supervision.

The message to parents is clear and simple. Help your children spend their money wisely. Prompt them to think about their wants and needs and the funds available to acquire them. If at some point you want to transfer some cash to them on a regular basis to make these acquisitions, do it and call it an allowance.

One parent I know, rather than give her fifteen-year-old a large cash allowance, gave her a credit card. The mother paid the bill, but the daughter was allowed to spend $500 on her clothes for the school year. With her mother's help she drew up a list of necessary purchases and shopped for them over a period of time. Both mother and daughter were pleased with the system. The same technique could be used with a checking account. The parent deposits to the checking account a certain amount while the child budgets and makes the expenditure. As pointed out before, giving a child cash (which a checking account is) does not insure that he will spend it properly. He can always write the check for a new stereo component rather than the clothes for which it was intended. So, even though the allowance is designed to instruct the child in the use of cash, it should not be given without strings.

A New York acquaintance gave his son $15,000 at the beginning of his sophomore year at college. The money was to cover some tuition, books, room, board and numerous other expenses. By February the money had been spent. My friend could not understand how this had happened. He had personally drawn up the budget and knew the funds to be sufficient. Having known the son for a number of years, I knew that he had not been well prepared to handle money. While not a spendthrift, he had never been given responsibility for managing his own finances. Whenever he needed money he asked for it and got it. The strain on the relationship between father and son was probably avoidable and unnecessary.

One of our most important responsibilities as parents is to educate our children in the use of money. Our goal should be to foster healthy and objective attitudes toward money and material wealth. Knowledge of our economic system coupled with the basic tools of personal finance, should allow our children to exploit the opportunities and develop their talents.

A senior officer of a large financial institution insisted that his son, at age twelve, get a job. His purpose was obviously not to generate income, the family was quite comfortable in that regard. The purpose was to educate the boy in the ways of American economic life. He wanted his son to appreciate how a business operates.

In this case the young man became a waterman, that is, he caught and sold the natural harvest of the Chesapeake Bay. As an independent businessman he maintained books, marketed his products, and invested his profits to purchase necessary equipment. The lessons learned were many and could fill a book themselves.

My friend's attitude towards his son's income was that since he earned it he could spend it. It is true as the boy grew older, more responsibility for personal purchases was shifted to him. In this sense his father did influence how the money was spent. He also admitted however, that his son developed the habit of spending somewhat impulsively. For a child his age he had a lot of money and if he ran out he knew where he could get more. Certainly, the nature of his job, and perhaps his own personality, affected his attitudes. His father, however, might have spent a little more time instructing his son on the expenditure of his hard earned income.

Another parent had a somewhat different approach. Her fourteen-year-old son earned about $80 a week as a gardener. She insisted that he save half his income and oversaw the expenditure of the other half. She even went so far as to call her son's employers to determine their satisfaction with his work. Some might consider this extreme, certainly her son thought so. However, depending on the child and other circumstances, it may be warranted. If your daughter is not asked back to babysit there may be a reason that would be worth knowing. A little feedback from your child's employer might be quite helpful.

THE FAMILY CIRCUS

5-23

"She has her Care Bear, Rainbow Brite,
Pound Puppy, My Little Pony, Cabbage
Patch Kid and Strawberry Shortcake,
but I can't find Chatty Patty."

One of the saddest aspects of contemporary American life is the commercial exploitation of our children. The younger the child the sadder it is. Through the medium of television marketers excite our children to demand essentially worthless products. Take the "Care Bears" as an example. To the preschool child the appeal of these cuddlesome creatures is overwhelming. The animation of television sets up a physical bond with the child that is almost real. When the child realizes that these soft little creatures can be purchased down at the local K Mart, her craving begins to match that of a mother's for her lost child. The bear, which is no different from other teddy bears, has been endowed with all the qualities that only Saturday morning television can instill. Your child, who normally would be content with a $5 bear, now requires one with a red heart glued to its rear end and costing $15. Mommy and Daddy can sense something is amiss here, but rather than deny their little precious they dutifully plunk down $15. Not surprisingly, a whole team of these little creatures begin to appear. How did this happen?

Where the Kids Come In

Why are we buying $5 teddy bears for $15? The simple answer is that the $15 bear is a $5 bear with $10 of advertising expense packed into it.

This technique is very common in adult products. A classic example was Smirnoff Vodka. By advertising the brand name, Heublein, the distiller could charge a premium over the price it charged on an unadvertised brand called Popov, even though the products were virtually identical. The appeal of the higher priced Smirnoff harks back to an old market saw, "You get what you pay for." The more expensive refrigerator is better than the less expensive one. While often true, it was not in the case of Smirnoff vodka. Nevertheless, the Heublein marketers were able to exploit this belief to their profit. While no one much cares whether vodka drinkers get hoodwinked by their vanity, the same indifference should not extend to our children.

While some might advocate the enactment of laws regulating children's advertising, a better course is to educate your child in the ways of the consumer world. Through the media children are presented a consumer candy store where myriad wants are arrayed dazzlingly before them. Virtually the entire spectrum is made of goods that promise a happier and better life. Rarely do you see the necessities of life advertised on television. One wonders what the effect of promoting green vegetables might be. Like an adult the child begins to associate his happiness with the acquisition of some product. But unlike the adult he has no experience or judgment to evaluate the relative worth of the product. If he is denied the toy, he becomes depressed. If given the toy, the behavior syndrome is reinforced. As they grow older the pattern continues. "Mom I just have to have that Benetton sweatshirt; everybody has one." Once exposed the compulsion to consume the product becomes relentless. How many products are bought and shelved or closeted forever? Like the compulsive eater the compulsive consumer acquires goods simply to satisfy a craving and not to satisfy a particular need.

A few years ago McDonald's had a TV advertisement showing a pre-teen brooding because his new baby sister was receiving all the adult attention. The enlightened father on seeing his son's depressed condition suggests they take a trip to McDonald's to alleviate the situation. The message is clear. If you have an emotional problem try eating your way through it, preferably at McDonalds. This type of thinking promotes compulsive behavior and is used extensively in the advertising media.

As children approach puberty, the obvious human appetite for advertisers to harness is the sex drive. The simple association of various products with a teenager's near addiction for the opposite sex becomes a powerful stimulus in product promotion. The teen, conditioned since childhood, perceives fulfillment and happiness in the purchase of a particular product. The buy is made and momentary satisfaction is achieved, only to be replaced by the craving for another product.

There is nothing particularly new about this behavior. The lure of the marketplace is as old as mankind. And mothers have always taught their daughters how to shop, haggle, and evaluate goods and people. But times have changed. Advertising techniques have advanced faster than our abilities to explain them. Mothers now work outside the home and cannot always supervise their children's television watching. The psychological subtlety of the advertising media circumvents even a mother's watchful eye. No longer can a child be protected from the market by just keeping him at home. The media is pervasive; the onslaught is continuous.

As the child grows, he develops an attitude toward personal fulfillment that is closely associated with material goods. The progression from Care Bears to Izod to Bill Blass to a BMW is perceptible. So strong is the good feeling associated with consumer buying that going shopping is a common cure for the momentary blues. It is not that the practice of consumption is wrong, on the contrary it is very necessary. What is wrong is our attitude toward it. There is nothing sadder than a teenager moping around because he cannot buy a new pair of "Reeboks" that he just has to have.

Like a corporation, individuals and families need to allocate financial resources wisely in order to maximize their potential. These allocations should be fairly objective and devoid of emotion. Most parents realize the priority demands on their income. Shelter, transportation, food, insurance and savings certainly come right off the top. Discretionary income is limited for just about everyone. Children should realize that these limits exist and, most probably, always will.

Among the many consequences of our consumerist attitude, probably none is more insidious than the measuring of self-worth by the level of one's income or attainment of material goods. Some of the problem stems from the widely held belief that the distribution of income is based on merit. Those who work hard and apply themselves will achieve monetary success. The corollary has to be that those who do not apply themselves will have less monetary success. This so-called merit system begins in school. There are A students, and there are C students. Many at each level work hard and apply themselves, but who gets the prizes? The A students. Even if the A student simply has a congenital gift for mastering certain academic subjects, he will be rewarded as if he were somehow responsible for the gift. Likewise, the C student who works doubly hard to overcome a personal handicap may not be recognized for his efforts. The A student begins to develop self-esteem; the C student does not. In the nonacademic business world, the prizes are monetary and the manifestation is material goods. The association between material goods and self-esteem becomes so enmeshed that an individual often cannot differentiate between them. The consequences can be devastating. When the subjective complexity of self-esteem is reduced to the simplicity of a consumer item then the murder of a young man for a Georgetown University warm-up jacket—an event which indeed took place on the streets of Baltimore in 1985—becomes understandable.

Although the above example is admittedly extreme, the importance of consumer goods to an American child's self-esteem is nevertheless very real. Some people are admired simply for the car they drive, the schools they attend, or the clothes they wear. As a consumer nation we measure the very subjective qualities of self-esteem by the very objective terms of material goods.

The problem a parent faces is breaking down this relationship. Regardless of your income your child should develop a high level of self-esteem. One way of doing that is by developing healthy objective attitudes towards money. If the child can understand the limits of the family income and the standard of living it will support, he should then be able to accept the material differences between himself and his peers. It is a mark of intellectual maturity to see through the material surroundings of an individual. A child should be able to see himself and his classmates in this manner.

This idea implies that there are other more meaningful qualities by which someone should measure themselves and others. What they are depends on your culture and the times. As a parent you know best what they are. I will say only that it is not the mindless acquisition of consumer goods and pandering to the advertising media.

There is a natural process by which we protect our children from material challenges to their self-esteem. We tend to live, and socialize within our economic class. Often times the homes in a neighborhood will be of similar value. The neighbors will buy the same model cars and the children will go to the local school. The material differences are minimized. The child's exposure to other economic classes is through TV, movies or a more affluent relative. It is not until college or work that the child comes into daily contact with people from differing economic circumstances. The ghetto mentality of his origins often leaves him ill-prepared for the economic diversity of American Society.

One very successful businessman expressed great concern that his children might not appreciate the benefits of their wealth. They appear to take their privilege far too much for granted. He is now a multimillionaire but he knows that the acquisition of his wealth was somewhat fortuitous. In other words he appreciates his good fortune and he wants his children to also. How does he do that?

First, he encourages them to work and earn money, not just at odd jobs around the house but as an employee for someone else. Second, he monitors closely their consumption. If his daughter wants an Esprit shirt for thirty dollars, he points out that the basic shirt is worth ten dollars and the next twenty dollars is for the name. So he funds the first ten dollars and she puts up the twenty dollars for the brand name from her savings account. It would be far easier just to give her the thirty dollars and be done with it. But he wants to teach his daughter value,and this is one way to do it.

As noted, his children already have savings accounts. He intends to have them buy shares of common stock for educational purposes. Following the progress of a company and identifying its products in the marketplace, will enhance his childrens' awareness of how American business operates.

ACTIVITIES

1. Give your children a cash allowance designed to cover certain expenditures which would otherwise be made by you. Write a contract and monitor those expenditures with your child.

2. Look into what your children are learning about consumerism in their schools. Many social studies courses in elementary and secondary schools now teach children how to be discerning consumers. If your children's school does not cover consumerism, talk to the principal. Perhaps the PTA could work to organize a consumer unit.

3. If your child is old enough, help him find a part-time job. There are many things to be learned in the work place, self-reliance and confidence, as well as deductions and taxes.

The following quiz was developed by Future Homemakers of America, Inc. as part of *Financial Fitness* by Carolyn Mulford a teen peer education program, sponsored by *Changing Times*, the Kiplinger magazine of personal finance. Take the quiz yourself first and check out your answers. Some of them are really tricky. Then give the quiz to your burgeoning teenagers. It will help them put into perspective their own spending and earning, now and in the future.

In the introduction to this program, it states: "If you're an average teenager, you already are spending more than $1,000 on yourself each year, much of it on clothes." Also cited is a recent study by the Teen-Age Research Institute which shows that an estimated $30.5 billion was spent by teenagers on themselves in 1986. There is no doubt that teenagers are avid consumers.

You may want to alert your children's high school to the availability of the *Financial Fitness* program. Basically, Future Homemakers of America members learn about money management skills. Then they use the financial fitness materials to teach their peers. For future information, contact: Future Homemakers of America, Inc. 1910 Association Drive, Reston, Virginia 22091, 703-476-4900.

FINANCIAL FITNESS QUIZ

Are you financially fit? Do you know what you need to know about earning, spending and saving money? Check your financial fitness by answering the following questions. Just write the letter of the correct answer in the blank to the right of each question.

1. By the time teenagers graduate from high school, approximately 8 out of 10 have had jobs.
   a. true   b. false   _____

2. The most common jobs for senior high school students are store clerk and fast-food restaurant worker.
   a. true   b. false   _____

3. In a lifetime of work, the average teenager can expect to earn
   a. $50,000-300,000   b. $300,000-700,000
   c. $700,000-$1,000,000
   d. more than $1 million.   _____

4. The national minimum wage is (fill in amount).   _____

5. Jill works 15 hours a week at $3.60 an hour. Jack works 12 hours a week at $4.20 an hour. Who earns more?
   a. Jill   b. Jack   _____

6. People who have plenty of money don't need a financial plan.
   a. true   b. false   _____

7. Research indicates that, on the average, teenagers spend approximately
   a. $500-1,000   b. $1,000-2,000   c. $2,000-3,000
   d. $3,000-4,000 on themselves each year.   _____

8. When making your personal finance plan, count only take-home pay as income.
   a. true   b. false   _____

9. Textbooks spell out exactly what percentage of income every teenager should spend on entertainment, food, clothing and school supplies.
   a. true   b. false   _____

10. Jack's take-home pay is $40 a week, and he saves $4. Bob's take-home pay is $70 a week, and he saves $6. Who saves a higher percentage of his income?
a. Jack   b. Bob   _____

11. A good sign of a product's quality is its price.
a. true   b. false   _____

12. Some products are less expensive at one time of year than another.
a. true   b. false   _____

13. Most teenagers spend
a. none   b. $1-15   c. $15-35   d. $35-50 of their parents' income on groceries and other household products each week.   _____

14. If apples are cheaper by the dozen, the best buy in apples would be a dozen.
a. true   b. false   _____

15. Store A is offering 20% off on its $35 running shoes. Store B is offering 25% off its $40 price for the same shoes. Which store offers the lower price?
a. Store A   b. Store B   _____

16. Approximately half of all American teenagers do not save money, even for something special.
a. true   b. false   _____

17. Because most banks charge fees for writing checks, it is better to pay bills with money orders.
a. true   b. false   _____

18. Charge cards are rarely issued to a minor.
a. true   b. false   _____

19. Bank credit cards usually charge a lower interest rate on overdue accounts than a bank would on a loan.
a. true   b. false   _____

20. If a savings account pays 6% interest compounded monthly, the annual yield is
a. 6%   b. 17%   c. 7%   d. 10%   _____

21. On the average, Americans save approximately
a. 2-5%   b. 5-10%   c. 10-15%   d. 15-20% of their after-tax income.   _____

22. A teenager is more likely to have a
a. checking account   b. savings account
c. credit card.   _____

23. Federal law states credit unions, banks and savings institutions must pay the same interest rates.
a. true   b. false   _____

24. Stocks and bonds are very good investments for teenagers because you don't have to pay taxes on dividends and interest.
a. true   b. false   _____

25. A bank will lend you $2,000 at 8% for two years to buy a car. The dealer will lend you the money at 7% for three years. If you want to pay as little interest as possible, from which should you borrow the money?
a. bank   b. dealer   _____

26. Two can live as cheaply as one.
a. true   b. false   _____

27. For every dollar earned by men, women earn
a. less than 70 cents   b. 70-80 cents
c. 85 cents to $1   d. more than $1.   _____

28. If you make a $2,000 Individual Retirement Account contribution drawing 7% interest, in 30 years it will be worth approximately
a. $5,000   b. 10,000   c. $15,000   d. $20,000   _____

29. In families headed by high school dropouts, the median family income is approximately two-thirds that of families headed by college graduates.
a. true   b. false   _____

30. If you drop out of school halfway through your senior year, you can get a job paying $140 a week. If you stay in school and graduate, you can get a job paying $180 a week. In two years, would you earn more working at $140 a week for 104 weeks (starting immediately) or at $180 a week for 86 weeks (starting after graduation)?
a. $140 for 104 weeks   b. $180 for 86 weeks   _____

Where the Kids Come In

1. **(a)** National surveys indicate 8 out of 10 seniors have held jobs during their high school years (see *When Teenagers Work: The Psychological and Social Costs of Adolescent Employment,* by Ellen Greenberger and Laurence Steinberg, Basic Books, 1986).

2. **(a)** National surveys indicate retail and restaurant jobs are the most common types of jobs held by teenagers (see reference above).

3. **(d)** A high school graduate will earn an estimated $1 million in a lifetime.

4. **($3.35 in mid-1987)** From 1981 until late 1987, the minimum wage has been $3.35. Check with your local employment office for current figures.

5. **(a)** Jill's hours (15 multiplied by her hourly wage ($3.60) equals $54 a week. Jack's hours (12) multiplied by his hourly wage ($4.20) equals $50.40 a weekly income $3.60 lower than Jill's.

6. **(b)** One of the purposes of a financial plan is to help make the best possible use of money, whether large or small amounts.

7. **(b)** These figures are based on statistics reported by Teen-Age Research Unlimited in the December 1986 issue of *American Demographics.*

8. **(b)** You should count all sources of regular or expected income including your take-home pay, allowance, payment for odd jobs, gifts of money you receive on your birthday or other holidays, interest on savings or investments, profits from your business.

9. **(b)** No textbook gives a detailed spending plan that fits everyone's needs.

10. **(a)** Jack's savings ($4) divided by his take-home pay ($40) show he is saving 10%. Bob is saving approximately 8.5% of his take-home pay.

11. **(b)** Price does not always determine quality. Many factors, including the cost of advertising, freight and overhead, are used in setting prices.

12. **(a)** Many products have sale seasons, and prices generally go down as new models—of cars, computers, clothing, etc.—enter the market.

13. **(c)** A 1985-86 Teen-Age Research Institute survey indicates that 12- to 15-year-olds spend approximately $20 for the family and 16- to 17-year-olds approximately $31.

14. **(b)** A dozen is not the best buy if some would be wasted.

15. (a) Store A will take off 20% (.20 × $35 = $7; $35 – $7 = $28). Store B will take off 25% (.25 × $40 = $10; $40 –$10 = $30). Store A's price is $2 lower than Store B's.

16. (a) The figures come from a study reported in "Premature Affluence: Do High School Students Earn Too Much?" by Jerald G. Bachman. Survey Research Center, University of Michigan, *Economic Outlook USA*, Summer 1983.

17. (b) Many banks charge no fees or minimal fees for checks. Money orders have a fee attached, and it's usually higher than checking account fees.

18. (b) Many local businesses, particularly department stores and gas stations, issue charge cards to minors, but usually only if their parents sign a statement taking responsibility.

19. (b) Bank credit cards usually carry very high interest rates— sometimes more than 20%. Bank loan rates usually are 5% to 10% lower than credit card rates.

20. (b) The monthly compounding of interest (adding the interest earned that month to the amount deposited so you draw interest on interest) increases the amount earned.

21. (a) In 1986, the personal savings rate was 3.8% of after-tax income. The rate in 1982 was 6.8%.

22. (b) A 1985-86 Teen-Age Research Institute survey reports that 74% have savings accounts, 17% have checking accounts and 12% have credit cards available to them.

23. (b) Rates may vary among all three and within any of the three.

24. (b) Age does not exempt anyone from paying taxes on dividends and interest, but teenagers usually pay lower rates because their total income is less than that of adults.

25. (a) Lenders figure interest in different ways for cars, but generally the shorter period will keep your total interest lower.

26. (b) Two people living together can live more cheaply than two people living independently, but not as cheaply as one.

27. (a) The Bureau of Labor Statistics reported women's earnings have risen from 61 to 62 cents of every dollar earned by men in the 1970s to 69 cents in the mid-1980s.

28. (c) If the interest rate remained constant at 7%, the interest added on each year would bring the total to approximately $15,000.

29. (a) The 1986 *Statistical Abstract of the United States* gives a median income of $14,849 for those who dropped out of high

school after one to three years. $22,418 for high school graduates and $37,147 for college graduates.

30. **(b)** The graduate would earn (86 × $180 = $15,480), $720 more than the dropout (104 × $140 = $14,560).

How did you do? Count one point for each correct answer.
Financially fit—26-30
In fair shape—21-25
Need to work out—16-20
Financially flabby—11-15
Help!—1-10

Part II

What To Do With What's Left

PROVIDING FOR THE FUTURE AND MAKING THE MOST OF TODAY One of the most worrisome aspects of life is the need to provide for ourselves. While we are young we can work and the problem is manageable. But after retirement our income must come from other sources, which usually include savings. Worry comes not only from deciding how much to save, but from how to invest those savings. Savings are accumulated by sacrificing consumption and limiting our lifestyle, doing without so something can be put aside. The anxiety comes from never knowing how much is enough. Should I save 5 percent of my income, 10 percent, or what? The investment itself becomes a source of concern because it involves risk: the risk of lost opportunity or the risk of a shaky financial venture.

We baby boomers have not been particularly good savers. There are a number of reasons for this habit. First, the Keynesian economists have created an environment that thrives on internal demand. Consumer spending represents 50 percent of our gross national product. If the consumer lets up, our economy stagnates. To stimulate the consumer, the government makes money available through transfer payments, government spending and low interest rates. This activity in turn stimulates the economy by creating more jobs and more demand, a little bit the way a firestorm sucks in oxygen to feed itself. Adding to the storm is the advertising media, which creates demand for new products. The pressures to spend your cash in America are enormous.

Another reason for our low savings rate has been inflation. When prices are rising, the tendency is to commit cash to goods that are expected to be more expensive later on. In such an environment some investments and the savings they represent lose value.

A third reason, tied to the first, is that the rising American standard of living is very expensive to finance. Americans constantly feel a need to buy bigger and better homes, cars, clothes and vacations. "Keeping up with the Joneses" is a very real force in some American lives. To be seen in an old car or outdated clothes is simply inconceivable to some people. Many Americans claim a desire to be rich; but what they really want is to appear rich as well, which brings us to a fourth reason.

The parents of many baby boomers lived through a vicious depression and traumatic world war. Financially and psychologically they are somewhat less secure than their children, and given their experiences, for good reason. They were, however, good savers. They bought homes, raised and educated their children, and invested their excess income. For the most part these investments have paid off handsomely because they have been held for a long period of time. Unfortunately, many young Americans view their parent's wealth as their own and see no reason to save. In some cases this assumption is valid but in others it is not. Finally, many baby boomers believe their company pension plans, social security and small savings will be enough to sustain their later years. Perhaps they will, but this point brings us back to how much savings is enough.

4

Financial Planning

"Dad, what's a rainy day?"

The easiest way to answer the question of how much you should save is to see a financial planner. With her help you can do some calculations that will project costs of living over the course of your life and, in turn, project your probable sources of income over the same period.

Such figures are only projections. Personal as well as economic circumstances can change rapidly; nevertheless projections must be made. They act as a benchmark to measure change. If inflation heats up, new projects may be necessary. If you lose your job or receive an unexpected windfall, the figures can be adjusted to reflect your changed circumstances.

At some point bringing other family members in on these projections may not be a bad idea either. Since the plan may affect your children, someone other than the parent should know about them. Children should be prepared for whatever responsibilities or windfalls may befall them.

Below is a simplified sample financial plan. Many insurance agents, banks and brokers will prepare such plans free of charge. But be careful, some are better than others, so do not hesitate to get more than one. Much of the planning is little more than the application of common sense. (When will you retire? Where will you live?) The value of the plan is to make sure all bases are covered and nothing is forgotten. The projections imply assumptions regarding future events like rates of inflation. If they change, a revised plan may be called for. Finally, the plan should quantify reality and expectations to insure that they are consistent.

Essentially the calculations take your current income and assets, and project their future value by adjusting for inflation and investment returns. These figures are then compared to a similarly adjusted Desired Retirement Income. Desired Retirement Income is usually around 60 percent of pre-retirement income. If the calculation indicates a shortage, a savings and investment plan is developed to make up the difference. All the following calculations use a 6 percent annual inflation rate and a 8 percent annual investment return and a 5 percent annual appreciation for real estate. We also assumed that John and Jerica will retire in twenty years and live for thirty years after retirement. The following statements of net worth and cash flow for John and Jerica Cloves are the basis for the calculations.

JOHN AND JERICA CLOVES
State of Financial Position As of December 31, 1984

ASSETS

Cash/Cash Equivalents
Checking account	$ 1,500
Money market mutual fund	30,000

Total Cash/Cash Equivalents	$ 31,500

Invested Assets
IRAs	$ 20,000
Cash value life insurance	30,000
Common stock portfolio	10,000
Vacation condominium	80,000

Total Invested Assets	$140,000

Use Assets
Automobiles	$ 20,000
Furnishings, personal items	50,000
Residence	150,000

Total Use Assets	$220,000
TOTAL ASSETS	$360,000

LIABILITIES AND NET WORTH

Liabilities

Car loan	$ 22,000
Commercial real estate mortgage	60,000
Residence mortgage	60,000

Total Liabilities	$130,000
Net Worth	$230,000

TOTAL LIABILITIES AND NET WORTH — $360,000

INCOME

Salaries after taxes	$ 55,000	
Condominium rental income	8,400	
Dividends and interest	2,500	
Net long-term capital gains	2,000	
Total inflows		$67,900

EXPENSES

Savings and Investments		$ 6,050
Fixed Expenses		
Condominium real estate expenses	$ 9,000	
Residence mortgage payments	15,400	
Life insurance premiums	500	
Auto insurance and umbrella liability policy premiums	1,000	
Total Fixed Expenses		25,900

Variable Expenses		
Food	$ 8,800	
Transportation	11,000	
Utilities/household expenses	4,400	
Clothes/personal care	2,860	
Medical/dental care	800	
Recreation/vacations	2,700	
Charitable contributions	2,200	
Miscellaneous	4,000	
Total Variable Expenses		36,760

Total Expenses	$ 68,710

		Present Value	Future Value
Step 1	Establish objectives and assumptions		
Step 2	Determine assets available	$ 91,000	
Step 3	Calculate future value of available assets from Step 2 adjusted for inflation and investment return		$ 424,147
	Calculate future value of real estate adjusted for inflation and investment return	$230,000	610,258
	Total future value of available assets		$1,034,405
Step 4	Estimated desired retirement income (about 52% of current income)	$ 34,850	
	Social Security and Pension Income	13,068	
	Net income needed	$ 21,782	
	Future value of net income needed for retirement adjusted for 5% inflation		$ 69,858
	Lump sum needed at retirement to provide desired income		$1,595,859
Step 5	Future value of assets available to provide desired income (from Step 3)		1,034,405
	Future value of additional funds needed to generate desired retirement income		$ 561,454
	Present value of additional funds needed to generate desired retirement income	$175,064	
Step 7	Annual savings needed to generate additional funds for annual income		7,205
	Percent of current income (7,205/67,900)		10.6%

I would suggest not spending too much time reconciling these numbers because the calculations can be done several different ways. A better approach would be to see a financial planner and reconcile your own family's numbers with her system.

ESTATE PLANNING

HERMAN JAMES UNGER

"Grandpa, they've been arguing
all afternoon about who's
going to get your pool table."

During a periodic review of his estate plan a client of mine wryly remarked, "All of these things will take place while I am in purgatory."

From our long relationship I knew his comment was not a statement of religious belief but an expression of his total indifference to events that would take place after his death. But this man dearly loved his wife and children and even in death he did not want to cause anxiety or discomfort to them. Hence, he arranged his affairs in such a fashion to minimize decision and conflict after his death.

His first act was to make an estate plan and his second one was to explain it in detail to his wife. The plan consisted of his will and a living trust. His will stated briefly that all his personal effects were to go to his wife if she were living and if not, to their three children. His will also provided for the distribution of insurance policies, pension and profit sharing plans, and IRAs.

The bulk of his financial assets were held in a revocable deed of trust, which he managed in conjunction with my bank. He had structured the portfolio to provide income for his wife after his death. The trust would continue throughout her lifetime and was then to be distributed outright to his children. Since the trust was not subject to probate, there would be no interruption of income to his wife as a result of his death. The terms of the trust provided for her well-being if she became incapacitated during her lifetime. The trustees were allowed to expend the entire sum for her benefit if the need arose. In fact, during her lifetime she could terminate the trust if she so desired. Although she could exercise complete control over the assets if she chose, she could also do nothing and the assets would be properly invested and the income paid to her on a regular basis.

His wife concurred in the estate plan and was a party to it. She would become a trustee of the trust at his death, as well as being co-personal representative, with our bank, of his estate. She knew where every bank account, insurance policy, and tax return was located. Although his death would be a great personal loss, it would not involve the anxiety associated with investment decisions, taxes, and estate settlement.

The question again arises as to how much the children should be told. Probably more than they usually are. In the case of my client their eldest daughter, who had recently married, was advised of their entire situation. The reason was simply that under certain circumstances she might be responsible for representing the family to trustees, doctors and others responsible for caring for her mother, father or both. She needed to be aware of the financial resources available for these responsibilities. Otherwise she might have needlessly worried whether there was enough money to provide for illness and other needs. Estate planning provides security for your children of all ages. Let them know you have done it.

ACTIVITIES

1. A number of camps have sprung up to teach children how to manage their money from a fairly early age. One such camp is Dollars and Sense, run by Smart Services Inc., 439 28th St., West Palm Beach, FL 33407. This financial camp offers children ages 10-15 a five-day minicourse on the fundamentals of money management. Conducted and created by Lois O'Connor and Paul Vattiat, financial consultants for Shearson Lehman Brothers, Inc. the camp has been operating for three years. It costs about $600, not including food and lodging. The camp's founder, Barbara S. Smart, is currently developing a board game called "Money Management Mania" and are writing a book called *The Dollars & Sense Guide to Fiscal Fitness*. For further information, call Barbara S. Smart, Smart Services, Inc., 305-655-2229.

2. Visit a financial planner and compare your actual situation with his recommendations. Review your own will and financial plans. If appropriate, tell your older children about your plans, especially if they are named as personal representatives or trustees. Powers of attorney should also be given to adult children, if appropriate, to provide legal continuity in the event of illness.

3. Help your child set up a budget of her own expenses and income. Project how much she'll need to save regularly to make a designated purchase. Monitor her progress and make a family occasion when the goal is reached.

4. There are two excellent board games you can play with your children to teach them about planning and money. They are *Life* (Milton Bradley) and *Monopoly* (Parker Brothers). There are also variations of *Monopoly* based on the streets of many American cities. Check out your local toy or book store.

5

Bonds
and
Stocks

"Mom, what *is* the stock market?"

Warren Shimmerlik is a vice president for Merrill Lynch Pierce Fenner & Smith. From his New York office overlooking the Hudson River he analyzes the domestic oil industry. Warren, as you would guess, makes a pretty good buck. But he isn't fooled by the level of his success. He still has to work for it. As he will tell you there is a great deal of difference between a dollar received for services rendered and a dollar received from a trust set up by one's grandfather. He also has some good ideas on teaching children about investments.

Projecting income and expenses is only half of the savings equation. The other half is how to invest the cash you save. What to invest in requires some thought and decision making, and since decisions imply right and wrong courses of action, there is some anxiety as well. Nevertheless, for all its complexity investment lends itself to common sense, which if applied, will ease anxiety by substituting predictability and confidence.

Warren and I agreed there are many rules you can follow when investing, some are better than others. One good one is to stick with what you can understand. If you make an investment be sure the numbers are clear and understood. Another is to assume a correlation between risk and reward. For example, if one bank is paying a higher interest rate on their savings accounts than another, assume there is more risk associated with the higher rate of interest. Believe there is a difference between speculating and investing even when they appear to be the same thing. For example, if you buy one hundred shares of IBM to pay for your two-year-old's college education, that is an investment. If you buy one hundred shares when he is a sophomore to pay for the next year's tuition, that is a speculation.

A third rule is to focus on cash. If you give someone cash, know when and how much cash you expect to get back. The more tenuous this relationship between the giving and receiving of cash, the riskier the investment. The form of repayment, dividends, interest, principal payments, whatever, does not matter as long as it puts cash back into your hands.

A corollary to this rule is that the more quickly the cash comes back the less risky the investment. Lending cash for a year is less risky than lending it for five years, because many adverse things can happen over time. But remember that less risky investments should pay less than more risky investments and that is where the trade off comes.

Rules for investment are not like the laws of physics. Sometimes exactly the opposite will happen, especially over short periods of time. Let's talk about some examples.

BONDS

Just about anything you purchase for cash with the expectation of receiving more cash in return can be considered an investment. At some point, however, the investment becomes a speculation. The purchase of a lottery ticket is not an investment even though cash is given in expectation that more cash will be returned, because the probability of getting any cash back is virtually nonexistent. On the other hand, if you buy a certificate of deposit at your local savings and loan, the probability of getting your cash back is extremely high, so the investment is one of very high quality. The probability is high because a reputable organization has contracted to use your cash for a fixed period of time and for a fixed amount of money (interest). This same high quality applies to other contractual obligations like bonds from a corporation. If the corporation fails to repay the cash you are due, a court proceeding will follow to liquidate the corporation's assets. For example, if you buy a five year General Electric 8 percent bond, here is how the repayment works. Remember: focus on cash.

You give $10,000 to General Electric on July 1, 1986 and receive a piece of paper saying GE will pay you 8 percent, each year for the next five. They further agree to make half the annual payment every six months. Here is how the cash flows back to you.

January 1, 1987	$ 400
July 1, 1987	400
January 1, 1988	400
July 1, 1988	400
January 1, 1989	400
July 1, 1989	400
January 1, 1990	400
July 1, 1990	400
January 1, 1991	400
July 1, 1991	10,400
Total	$14,000

So, after five years you have received back $14,000; but note, you received the first $400 after only six months. That $400 payment, and the ones that follow, can be reinvested to earn even more money. This reinvestment of the cash interest payment is known as compounding interest, one of the most powerful concepts of investment. Of course, you do not know what rate you will reinvest the money at, so you cannot really tell what your total return will be after five years. Each six months the rate may be different. However, as planners for the future we must make projections on that reinvestment rate and a bond salesman will happily do that for you. But it is important to remember that once we go into projections we are back into probability. Nevertheless, we should make these projections for planning purposes and compare them to other investments.

So General Electric bonds are a very high quality investment because the cash is paid back to you on a regular basis and under an agreement that is legally binding. The fact that General Electric is a financially strong company adds to the quality of the investment. How does one know whether a company is financially strong?

Independent bond rating agencies such as Standard & Poor's and Moody's, rank various bonds in order of their probability of default. For example, the highest quality bonds are rated AAA and have a lower probability of default than do single A's. Moody's and Standard & Poor's conduct an in-depth analysis of each issuing corporation to determine its level of credit risk. A committee determines the eventual rating and since neither agency is involved in trading bonds, the decision is deemed to be impartial. In fact, so admirable is the record of these agencies that many regulatory commissions will direct banks and insurance companies to abide by their ratings when making investments. In practice, since bond defaults are relatively rare, the importance of the rating is its effect on yields and prices. A low quality bond will yield more cash or cost less than a high quality one, thereby reflecting the higher risk.

THE STOCK MARKET

There are other types of investment that pay back cash on a regular basis but do not have the contractual relationship that General Electric bonds do. Common stocks are a good example. Some stocks have paid dividends for fifty years. The probability that they will continue to do so is apparently very high. But they are under no legal obligation to do so. The amount and frequency of those dividends is strictly at the discretion of management. Their motive in paying dividends is to get people (savers) to give them cash to buy assets, which they will use to make more cash.

As you can see, common stocks by their very nature are more risky than bonds. Nevertheless, when you look at the long term record, the returns seem worth the risk.

Under the heading of the stock market, the Library of Congress card catalogue lists hundreds of volumes. What can I say in a few pages to help you explain to your children a subject which provokes so much interest. Well, there may be an equal number of books on the automobile and its underlying engineering principles. Nevertheless the internal combustion engine and the mechanical drive mechanism that propels 90 percent of our cars and trucks are conceptually quite simple. An explosion takes place in a chamber causing pressure, which is transferred to the wheels by a series of gears that cause motion. The explosion is caused by the rapid oxidation of gasoline ignited by a spark. If any of these elements is missing, the car won't work. So what about stocks?

The stock market is a place where stocks are bought and sold for cash using an auction method. Stocks themselves are pieces of paper which are evidence of ownership in the assets of a company. Whoever owns the stock of IBM owns the assets of the company. The assets, and therefore the stock, have value because properly used they produce cash. If the asset is oil, it can be sold to produce cash. If the assets are machines, they can produce goods that can be sold for cash. Sometimes, as in a bank, the assets are nothing more than pieces of paper representing IOUs from people and corporations. Nevertheless, the IOUs if they are paid off will result in cash. Determining how much cash will be generated by the assets of a company is the job of management. The more tenuous the relationship between the assets and the cash they produce, the more difficult it becomes to put a price on the stock.

If we only bought stocks to produce cash dividends, life would be much simpler. Instead some of our ancestors took their stocks down to a place called Wall Street in lower Manhattan and started trading their stocks back and forth. Not unlike a bunch of boys with a fistful of baseball cards, some of our forebears thought that trading stocks was more fun than simply owning them. Of course when you trade stocks you trade for cash, but people who buy and sell stocks will normally have most of their money in stock, and from a distance swapping stocks will appear little different in concept than swapping baseball cards. We know of course that some baseball card collections are better than others, and the difference is usually attributed to shrewd trading or the ability of the trader to foresee the rise of individual players.

So we have two things. We have stocks which we value because they produce cash for us, and we have the trading game on Wall Street where we swap them back and forth trying to find the Gary Carters and Daryl Strawberrys! One must always try to separate these aspects of stock ownership in order to maintain objectivity. And I say *try* because when the game is well played the distinction becomes blurred. However, if one does not maintain this objectivity, appearances can be costly. Going back to our car analogy for a second, if the car does not work you can put it in neutral, push it down a hill and for awhile it may look like a car, but with no operating engine it is nothing more than three thousand pounds of steel headed for disaster. Stocks can act the same way. For a while they look like good investments that will eventually throw off cash, but they also may be pieces of junk headed for disaster.

Like the used car market we have a stock market where people presumably trade their clunkers for a peach. The accessibility and efficiency of the stock market is one of the factors that lowers the risk of buying stock. The knowledge that someone somewhere will buy your stock back from you is a very comforting feeling. How many times have you bought something and said, "I wish I could get my money back." Well, the stock market lets you do that up to a point. Prices change and you may have to sell for less than you paid. Nevertheless this ability to redeem your investment, or the liquidity provided by the stock market, enhances the attractiveness of stocks for investment purposes. The problems arise when investors attempt to take advantage of the changing prices.

As I said before, we buy stocks because we hope to receive cash dividends. Further if the company's management has any moxie those dividends will grow. Look at the dividends provided by Exxon over the pasts few years.

Year	Dividend Per Share	Number of Shares, $10,000 Would Buy At Annual Average Price in 1982	Total Dividend
1982	3.00	357	1,071
1983	3.10	357	1,106
1984	3.35	357	1,195
1985	3.45	357	1,231
1986	3.60	357	1,285
Total			5,888

Compared to our bond example you can see that over a long period of time, if the dividends keep growing, you are going to get more cash back from $10,000 invested in Exxon than $10,000 invested in the General Electric Bond. But remember, Exxon is under no legal obligation to repay your $10,000 or pay you any dividends. In theory, as owners of the company, you and the other stockholders will fire the management if they do not create the profits to enhance your investment. This is precisely the argument and strategy that T. Boone Pickens and other corporate raiders have used to take over corporations and reap massive profits by reorganizing companies.

Talking about corporate raiders is a good place to begin talking about the stock market as opposed to stocks themselves. First, in order to maintain objectivity let us remember a few things. The stock market is an auction market, which means that prices are set by people constantly working out offers to sell, and bids to buy, various amounts of stock. On the floor of the exchange an auctioneer, called a specialist, organizes this confusion by bringing the buyers and sellers together and establishing a price. Like any market if there are more sellers than buyers, it will tend to depress the price of the stock. Likewise if there are more buyers than sellers, it will tend to increase the price. The important thing to remember is that it is the supply and demand for the stock that changes the price. If IBM stock drops 10 points you can assume people are selling a lot of stock compared to the amount being bought. Sometimes a major piece of news will so affect the price of the stock that trading will stop and the price will be adjusted by the specialist. Often this happens overnight.

Many people believe that these changes in stock prices are the reason you buy stocks. They believe that investing in stock is based on the ability to predict these changes. The better you predict them the richer you will be. This is precisely where the investing game becomes a little hairy. Because what you then need to predict is why people will tend to buy stocks rather than sell them. If everyone buys stocks simply hoping prices will go higher, the game begins to look a little like musical chairs. Whoever is out of position, or the last to buy, when everyone sits down, or sells, is the loser. This is great fun at childrens' parties but no way to invest your money.

Going back to our Exxon example, if you buy the stock to collect the cash dividends, you should not care too much what happens to the stock price. If the cash dividends are great enough they will, over time, cover your cost and provide a return equal to or better than less risky investments. Nevertheless you may notice one day while you are depositing your dividend checks that the stock is much higher than the day you bought it. Even though you like getting the cash dividends, you think perhaps you should sell the stock and do something else with the money.

And maybe you should, but it is hard to tell. After all, if Exxon is going to pay higher and higher cash dividends maybe you should keep it. Or, if those cash dividends are not going to grow maybe you should sell. This is the point where financial analysts and portfolio managers begin to earn their salaries.

The job of the financial analyst is to analyze the financial statements of a company and determine when and how much money it will make with the assets it has to work with. This analysis is a complex process and the best analysts usually have been doing it for a lifetime. A good analyst is worth paying for. When you open an account at your local broker, check to see what analysts he has access to. The commission you pay your broker for buying a stock is compensation for access to this first-rate analysis. But remember an analyst's report is not a crystal ball for telling future stock prices. Normally an analyst will focus on a company's financial fundamentals. A well run company may not always be a timely investment. Factors beyond the control of a company's management may limit its short term investment potential. Returning again to our Exxon Stock, let's look at its price action for selected periods of time.

Exxon Stock Price Range		
	High	Low
1980	44	26
1981	41	29
1982	32	24
1983	39	28
1984	45	36
1985	55	44
1986	74	48
1987	50	31

Some times are better than others to own the stock, even though the cash dividend has been increasing. Why is this so? Well remember our auction market. During the period 1980–1984 enough owners sold stock to cause the price to decline. Why did they sell? For many different reasons to be sure, but logic tells us that many decided their cash would be better invested elsewhere.

THE MONEY MASTERS This evaluation of alternative investments is the job of portfolio managers. Should you buy the General
Electric bond, the Exxon stock, or the certificate of deposit down at the
local bank? Or how about a vacation home or gold? There are a couple
of things to remember when making this evaluation. The wisdom of a
particular investment depends upon future events. And nobody can
foretell the future, even though we often celebrate successful individuals as if they had such powers. The truth is that risk is present with any
investment and so we become like quantum physicists and are left with
probability to predict future events.

We know that riskier investments should provide higher returns.
But if the probability of that return is low, then the risk may not warrant the investment. Furthermore, assigning probabilities to future investment returns is a very subjective business. This subjectivity is
caused by the unlimited possible outcomes and, most important,
time. To receive 10 percent on your cash in twelve months is not the
same as receiving 10 percent in two years. And 6 percent in six months
may be better than 10 percent in 12 months. At any rate, one must assign some sort of probability as to which investment will perform best.
At the layman's level this may amount to little more than an instinc-
tive guess. But those instincts should not be underrated. I have seen
many nonprofessional investors with excellent investment instincts,
developed over a lifetime of managing their own portfolio. At the professional level probability decisions are buttressed with vast amounts
of historical and projected data. But this data is often used simply to
justify a preconceived attitude. Another word for these instincts is
judgment. And good judgment is worth paying for. Most individuals
in any craft or profession will develop a second sense that is often
worth more than the most elaborate studies, proving again that the
human mind is the best computer of all.

Warren Buffet, one of the so-called money masters celebrated in
John Trains' book of the same name, is elsewhere quoted as saying that
if an investment is so complex he cannot understand it, he rejects it.
This is a good rule. Even though a few successful investments may pass
you by, at least your expectations will stay intact.

It is important to remember that these probabilities we are discussing are subjective in nature. If you throw a die you know that the probability of any particular number coming up is one out of six. Or if you
have a baby that the probability of having a girl is .4976. But when you
assign a probability that the stock market will go up by 20 percent next

year that outcome is only one among many. Lets look at some numbers: Some of the best years in the stock market were:

	1928	+43 percent
	1933	+54 percent
	1945	+36 percent
	1954	+52 percent
	1975	+37 percent
	1985	+30 percent
The worst years were:		
	1931	−43 percent
	1937	−35 percent
	1941	−11 percent
	1974	−26 percent

The average annual return is about +10 percent.

So you might say the best I can do is +54 percent, the worst −40 percent but probably +10 percent. But that's not quite true. The best and worst years may yet be ahead of us. And, most important, these outcomes are not random. They do not all have the same probability of occurring. The number of very bad and very good years is small.

STOCKS VS. BONDS   Now before we get lost in the wonderland of believing that we can predict the stock market, let us recall a few rules. The first is that in the long run, say fifty years, stocks will outperform bonds. And in the same time period bonds will outperform certificates of deposit. So if you are looking for the best return, you will buy stocks and never consider the alternative. However, as we have seen, stocks can be volatile and this volatility, while unavoidable, can be nerve wracking. Ah, but you say, I am wrong. You can sell your stocks when they are high and buy them back when they are low, which brings us back to whether we should sell our Exxon stock.

If our financial analyst confirms that the future earnings power of the company is permanently impaired (and you believe him) then probably the stock should be sold regardless of price. Barring this situation, the best question to ask may be, "What will you do with the money?" If you know a stock that will produce even more cash as a percentage of your investment, then perhaps you should sell the Exxon and buy the new stock. But remember the probability of receiving cash from the new stock may be lower than the probability of receiving a smaller amount of cash from Exxon, and further down the road to boot. These are definitely risks to consider. You may also have to pay taxes if the Exxon is sold. Taxes remember are always paid in cash.

Finally you may note that because your Exxon stock has risen so rapidly, the amount of future cash paid out as a percentage of your investment seems less than it was a few years ago. Therefore, you decide to sell a portion of your holdings. Only after a period of time will you know whether you were right to sell all or a portion of your holding. Probably you will have been better off to hold, especially if the period of time is a long one. But if you slept better during the period because you sold, then perhaps you made the best decision.

ACTIVITIES

1. One of the easiest ways to study the stock market is to develop a "paper portfolio" with your child, monitor its progress, and calculate the return. The stocks can be selected on any convenience basis, for example familiarity with the company's products. Annual reports can be read and discussed.

2. Encourage your local high school to have a corporate treasurer address a class discussing stocks and investments. Ideally this would be a publicly held company whose annual reports are available to the class.

3. Buy your child some common stock or help her buy it from her part-time job and let her monitor its activities in the financial press and the company's annual report. Choose a stock which the child can identify through its products.

6

Real Estate, Gold and Stamps

"Dad, I have a great idea. Let's buy a house at the beach. Then we wouldn't have to pay for our vacation."

I mentioned earlier that if you sold your Exxon stock you could reinvest in gold or a vacation home. We could include rare coins, stamps, and other collectibles among these alternative investments. Just for the record let us look at the performance of some of these investments.

	Compounded Annual Return for:					
	15 Years	Rank	10 Years	Rank	5 Years	Rank
U.S. coins	18.8	1	16.3	1	11.4	3
Oil	13.9	2	3.0	13	(11.8)	14
U.S. stamps	13.6	3	11.8	3	(1.3)	12
Gold	11.9	4	9.2	8	6.8	7
Silver	10.3	5	9.7	6	4.0	9
Treasury Bills	9.2	6	10.2	5	8.5	6
Old masters	9.2	7	9.7	6	9.5	5
Stocks	8.6	8	13.9	2	24.1	1
Bonds	8.7	9	9.7	7	19.7	2
Chinese ceramics	8.3	10	11.3	4	3.4	11
Housing	8.2	11	7.4	10	4.8	8
CPI	6.9	12	6.5	11	3.5	10
U.S. farmland	6.3	13	1.5	14	(7.8)	13
Foreign exchange	4.6	14	4.1	12	6.8	7
Diamonds	4.1	15	8.9	9	10.2	4

Source: Salomon Brothers Investment Policy publication, June 8, 1987.

These numbers indicate that a great deal of money can be made owning some of these items. But before we get too excited by these returns let us remember that some of these investments produce no cash.

REAL ESTATE

To be sure you can purchase cash-producing real estate which, like good stocks, can appreciate in value. However, one of the main disadvantages in owning real estate is its lack of liquidity. The purchase of even a small amount of real estate is cumbersome, compared to bonds or stocks. Direct ownership also involves management responsibilities. If you buy a vacation home you will need to maintain and rent it. In addition, direct ownership entails unlimited liability in the event that you are sued. The successful investment returns that many Americans have sustained in their own homes has led them to purchase additional real estate. But to own the home one lives in is much different from owning investment property. The latter in effect becomes a small business with all the risks and rewards that entails.

Real estate as an investment has been one of the great success stories of post-World War II America. The inherent desire to own one's home is an integral part of the so-called American Dream. While that goal has been realized by many Americans, another somewhat unexpected benefit has accrued to homeowners, a fat return on their investment. Rising real estate prices have increased the net worth of virtually every American homeowner. Rising prices in the real estate industry are not unique; the price of just about everything has gone up. The difference in home ownership is that unlike other necessities houses have a fairly long life and more important, banks will lend you up to 90 percent of their value to make a purchase. This borrowing power, or leverage, is the key to the fantastic returns on real estate investments.

YOUR TAX ADVANTAGES ANALYSIS
OF A SINGLE-FAMILY RENTAL PROPERTY

INCOME AND EXPENSE PROJECTIONS

Purchase price		$75,000.00
Down payment (7%)		−5,000.00

Mortgage		$70,000.00

Adjustable-rate mortgage (ARM) at 9.5%, 10.10 loan constant, 12.5% interest cap

Scheduled gross annual income ($750 × 12)		$ 9,000.00

Less estimated annual expenses		−1,307.50
Real estate taxes	$937.50	
Insurance	95.00	
Water and sewer	75.00	
Advertising	100.00	
Miscellaneous	100.00	
	$1,307.50	

Cash flow before debt service ($9,000.00 − $1,307.50)		$ 7,692.50
Less debt service ($589.17 month × 12)		− 7,070.00
Pretax flow		$ 622.50

Yield: 12% ($622.50/$5,000 down payment)

ESTIMATED TAX SAVINGS

You save two ways on April 15th.
First, your $622.50 pretax cash flow is
fully sheltered. If you're in the 33
percent tax bracket, that's equivalent
to a 17.9 percent return. Second, you
get a tax deduction of $1,199.50. That
helps reduce your adjusted gross
income. Here's how your deductions
add up to savings:

Gross annual income	$ 9,000.00
Less operating expenses	(1,307.50)
Less mortgage interest	(6,710.00)
Less depreciation*	(2,182.00)
Total tax deductions	$ 1,199.50

*Depreciation is calculated on
purchase price of $75,000, assigning 20
percent of price to land and 80 percent
of price to house. Land is not a
depreciable asset.

So successful and prolonged has been the rise in real estate prices that
real estate investment has become somewhat of a cottage industry.
Many people who would be leery about buying one hundred shares of
IBM stock for fear of stock market volatility, happily borrow $100,000
to buy a vacation home on the assumption that its value will increase
fairly quickly.

In addition to rising prices and easy loans, there has been favorable
tax treatment. The numbers on all this are pretty straight forward as the
chart below indicates.

According to these numbers, real estate investment almost looks
like a free lunch. Since we do not believe in such things, let us see what
could go wrong. A reversal of any of the factors that make real estate an
attractive investment could cause a problem. First, if the cash income is
insufficient to pay the mortgage, forced sale could result. Second, if
prices decline, the investment obviously becomes a loser. Third, if the
deductibility of real estate mortgage interest changes, the cash flow on
your investment could decline.

Borrowing money to buy something that is going up in price is an easy way to make money. Real estate is no different. Our tax laws and bank lending policies make it even easier. Nevertheless, its success depends on rising prices, which at some point should peak out. When they peak and at what price are the crucial questions. But that is true of most investments.

GOLD AND STAMPS

Earlier I suggested that when making an investment you should focus on cash. This is especially true of gold, stamps, and other collectibles. Remember, you will not receive any cash dividends or interest from gold or stamps. If you buy a $50 U.S. Eagle for $450, you will never see your cash until you sell it. The traditional attraction of gold is that unlike wheat and some other commodities it is extremely durable, and weathers the ages about as well as anything. Also gold, especially national coins like the Eagle and Maple leaf, can be bought and sold virtually anywhere without associated assaying costs. Unlike copper, you can exchange a large number of dollars for a relatively small amount of gold. Gold also has an increasing commercial demand in our high tech world because of its inherent physical qualities. Traditionally, gold has been the reserve currency of the world. If countries cannot negotiate trade with their own currency, gold is an acceptable alternative. More recently certain national currencies from time to time have played this reserve roll, such as the British pound and the American dollar. Nevertheless, many knowledgeable economists maintain that gold will again play a central role in the world's financial order.

Today most investors look to gold as a hedge against inflation. When other national currencies begin to lose their value, gold begins to appreciate. Note the graph.

DIVERSIFICATION

A final note on diversification: common sense tells you not to put all your eggs in one basket. Investments should consist of a mix—some certificates of deposit, some bonds, some stocks, perhaps a little gold and

The Price of Gold

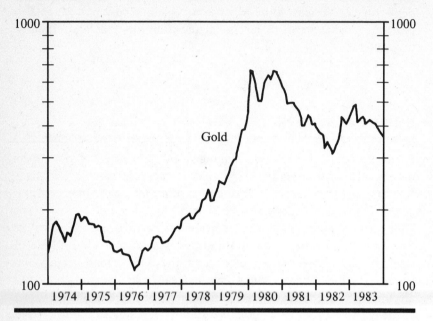

real estate. The purpose is to make money under all conditions and to stabilize the value of your portfolio. This is good advice but it does have its drawbacks. If you make a dollar in stocks only to lose it in your gold holding, little has been gained. The construction of your portfolio should reflect the risks and probabilities we have discussed.

ACTIVITIES

1. Encourage schools to have a local real estate salesman address a class on how local deals are put together. He could explain the interaction among broker, banker, buyers and sellers. A well prepared class could make for a very interesting session.

2. Find objects in the home that may have appreciated such as antiques, china, paintings and the like. Check a local auction catalog to see if you can find their current value. Use them as examples to discuss the value of collectibles as an investment.

3. Visit a local art gallery and discuss the investment as well as the aesthetic value of the collections.

4. A stamp or coin collection is an excellent way to learn about the value of these collectibles.

5. A new board game, called "Tycoon," could teach your children much about wheeling and dealing in the world of real estate. It's available for $20 at all F.A.O. Schwarz and Compleat Strategist stores.

6. "Monopoly" and "Advance to Boardwalk" are good real estate strategy games.

THE QUIGMANS

"... And then the evil S.E.C. placed a lien on his assets, and he was never to be seen again. ..."

7

Financial Services

"But, Mom, I don't want to put my birthday money in the bank!"

To what extent should children be exposed to the world of financial planning and investments? Probably no more than they want to be. However, if asked, parents should have a basic understanding of how major financial services are dispensed in the United States.

People with financial assets often will use a third party to manage their portfolios. Their reason for doing so is to have professional assistance in achieving their investment objectives. Investment counselors, stockbrokers, and bank trust departments provide such services. While you can hire someone to achieve your investment objectives, you must decide what those objectives are yourself. That responsibility is as personal as the right to vote. Similarly, no one else can set the level of risk necessary to achieve those objectives.

For example, if someone asked me to double his money in ten years that would be quite easy. A high quality zero coupon bond can be purchased today for $5,000 that will be worth $10,000 in ten years. But if someone asked me to double his money in six months, I would need to speculate in the stock or options markets with a high probability of failure. Nevertheless, achieving investment objectives at the least possible risk is the job of the portfolio manager. These money managers, as they are sometimes called, come in all shapes and sizes. Families should know the difference between them.

FINANCIAL PLANNING

Certified Financial Planners (CFPs) are designated as such by the International Board of Standards and Practices for Certified Financial Planners (IBCFP) in Englewood, Colorado. Essentially CFPs have completed a rigorous course of study and passed a series of six examinations over the course of 2 1/2 years. In addition CFPs must have three years of related work experience in financial planning.

At present, many CFPs are associated with a provider of financial services. For instance, in addition to being a CFP one might be an insurance salesman, a stockbroker, or a banker. Often the financial planning you receive from such an individual will be provided without charge as an enticement to purchase a basic service, like common stocks or insurance. It behooves one to be aware of these potential conflicts of interest because they could bias the advice you receive. If you visit a CFP who also sells insurance, do not be surprised if he discovers that you are underinsured. Many insurance professionals will have the designation ChFC (Chartered Financial Consultant) and CLU (Chartered Life Underwriter). To receive these titles the individual will have completed four or five years of advanced study through the American College in Bryn Mawr, Pennsylvania.

BANKERS

Certainly the most common form of investment in America is the savings account. Savings banks take in money through one door (savings accounts) and lend it out through another (mortgage loans). The difference between what they pay the saver for his deposit, and charge the borrower for his mortgage loan, is their profit. There are two risks the banker faces. One is that the rate difference just described may become unfavorable, meaning that he may have to pay depositors more than he can charge borrowers. The other is that all the depositors may want their money back at the same time. Since the banker has lent out most of the money, he may not be able to meet their demand. If either of these conditions persists for any length of time the bank will fail. In the wake of bank failures in the 1930s the federal government promised to insure each bank depositor to the amount of $100,000. Thus investing in a federally insured savings account appears to be a riskless investment. If this again appears to be a free lunch, and you do not believe in such things, you are right. What the government has promised to give you back is the same number of dollars you put in. It does not guarantee the value or purchasing power of those dollars. This latter quality will be maintained by the interest rate you receive. Whether that rate will be sufficient is up to you, the saver, to decide.

STOCKBROKERS

I have known a number of people who harbor ill feeling toward their former stockbrokers. In truth the ill feeling is usually not the fault of the broker. The usual cause is unrealistic expectations on the part of the investor. To be sure there are unscrupulous stockbrokers who promise virtually impossible returns. But unscrupulous people populate every business and profession. The broker is after all a salesman. He will put the best possible face on his product to encourage your purchase and win his commission. He may need that commission to pay his rent; and hence, he may be eager to sell you what he may not be willing to buy himself. The situation just described is more likely to happen when an individual is managing his own portfolio and using the broker as a source of advice. In such cases, the broker may have no idea what the individual's entire portfolio consists of and can only promote individual stocks unrelated to any over all investment strategy. Under such conditions, if unknown to the broker, a person invests half his savings in one stock and it declines by 50% thus wiping out 25% of the individual's savings, the broker can hardly be blamed.

An alternative would be to give the broker full discretion to buy and sell stocks in your portfolio. I have seen a number of such arrangements with wide ranging results. Many of the shrewdest money managers in the world are stockbrokers and their clients are much the richer for their skills. On the other hand, I have seen bunglers who have ruined portfolios through indiscriminate trading. But how does one select a good broker? It's not easy. A good comparison might be selecting an automobile mechanic. Many people believe that automobiles and stocks are equally confusing and approach both with fear and trepidation. My first comment would be that if you are fearful of the risk associated with stock investments you probably should not be making them, for unlike auto repairs, you do not have to invest in stocks if you do not want to.

Second, if you feel obligated to make stock investments for yourself or others, do some homework. Go to the local library and read. There are many excellent advisory services which are normally available. A good one to start with is *Value Line*.

Having begun with a caveat regarding the use of stockbrokers, let me continue by pointing out what a fabulous asset they are when properly used. One of the best in the business is Dick Greene of Merrill Lynch. From his Boston office, Dick can plug his client into a universe of investments that includes a product for every strategy and a risk commensurate with every objective, a short list follows:

Products	Strategies	Services
U.S. Treasury Bills	Buying on margin	Credit Management
U.S. Government Agency Bonds	Selling Short	Insurance
Corporate Bonds	Option Buying	Portfolio Management
Preferred Bonds	Option Writing	Financial Planning
Insured Certificates of Deposit	Futures Trading	Real Estate Services
Municipal Bonds		Securities Research
Common Stocks		
Convertible Bonds		
Zero Coupon Bonds		
Mutual Funds		
Precious Metals		

Source: Merrill Lynch.

You name it and he's got it. Not only does he have the product, he has the experts to analyze and prepare recommendations regarding its purchase. In discussing the use of brokers Dick was careful to point out that a broker is not for everyone. An individual should have reached a specific level of net worth prior to considering equity investments. Even then a minimum amount of risk capital is required before establishing an account. Most important, a person must know the level of risk he is comfortable with. A broker after all is not a psychologist. He cannot measure perfectly the sophistication or risk profile of his clients. Nor does he always have the time or inclination to educate his client in the nuances of various investments.

A broker might be viewed as a specialized, well honed tool. If properly used he will help you achieve your investment objectives in ways you never could on your own. But if you lack the skill or confidence to use the tool properly, you may well be better off having someone else do your bidding for you.

Finally, investment bankers are usually first to develop new products to meet new situations. For example, in 1985 they perceived a great demand for mutual funds of stocks from foreign countries, designed to take advantage of a falling U.S. dollar. In a short time they created Korean, Italian, Norwegian and other funds which were quickly snapped up by the marketplace.

INVESTMENT COUNSELORS

Investment counselors normally will take operational control of a portion of an individual's financial assets and manage them in accordance with a specific investment objective. The investments are usually a single type such as common stock, commodity futures, or real estate. The investment counselor may charge a direct fee for his services, often based on a percentage of the assets value. A round figure for investment counselors dealing in common stocks is 1 percent per year. If you have a $500,000 portfolio, the annual fee would be $5,000. Since investment counselors rarely have the capability to take physical possession of the stocks or bonds, a custodian of some sort, a bank or brokerage firm, is also required.

The primary advantage of using an investment counselor is the personalized service. If you retain an investment counselor his reputation for competence has been established and is therefore a known quantity. He will structure your portfolio to meet your objectives given his particular method and strategy. He will periodically report on his performance and if it is found to be unsatisfactory, the relationship can be terminated.

At the institutional level huge multibillion dollar pension funds will use several investment counselors. Their selection has become a business unto itself. The people who advise on which money manager to use are referred to as investment consultants. Consultants measure the performance of various managers and make recommendations on which should be retained and which fired.

TRUST DEPARTMENTS

A vast amount of American wealth is held and managed in bank trust departments. The popularity of trust departments stems from three factors. First, banks are highly regulated. Various state and federal auditors insure compliance with myriad regulations designed to prevent speculation and fraud. Second, trust departments have a reputation for conservative investment practices. While this reputation may be less deserved today than it once was, the perception persists. Finally, trust departments provide a unique service in that they alone among institutions can act as a trustee. A quick definition here will help. A trustee is an individual or a bank who takes legal possession of property and manages it, in accordance with an agreement, for the benefit of someone else. Banks also act as custodian for assets managed by others such as investment counselors, brokers, and mutual funds. People establish trusts for many reasons, most commonly to provide professional management and administration for financial assets under a recognized contractual arrangement, to insure privacy by avoiding the exposure of a publicly probated estate, to alleviate loved ones from the burden associated with managing financial assets, to insure that future events (like a marriage) do not frustrate plans for the eventual distribution of ones assets, and to protect minors and to avoid taxes.

For example, President John Kennedy's will established trusts for the benefit of his wife Jacqueline.

> 1. If my wife, JACQUELINE B. KENNEDY, survives me, then I give, devise and bequeath . . . unto my Executors and Trustees hereinafter named, In Trust, nevertheless, for the benefit of my said wife, to invest, reinvest and keep the same invested, and to collect and receive the rent, income and profits therefrom, and after deducting all proper reserves and expenses, to pay to my said wife, in each calendar year, all of the net income thereof; such payments to be made in semi-annual or sooner installments, as my Trustees in their sole discretion may determine.

The Kennedy will, which ran to ten pages, included many provisions which governed the execution of the trust. They included provisions for minor children and distributions from principal. Tax planning was also clearly evident in his will.

While Kennedy chose to appoint family members as trustees and executors, he could have chosen a lawyer, friend, or bank to carry out his will.

> I hereby nominate, constitute and appoint my wife, JACQUELINE B. KENNEDY, and my brothers, ROBERT F. KENNEDY and EDWARD M. KENNEDY, as Executors of, and Trustees under, this my Last Will and Testament; and if for any reason at any time any one of them does not qualify or is unable or unwilling to serve as such Executor or as such Trustee, I hereby nominate, constitute and appoint the following, in the order named, as Executrix or Trustee of this my Last Will and Testament (as the case may be) to fill any such vacancy: my sisters, EUNICE K. SHRIVER, PATRICIA LAWFORD and JEAN KENNEDY.

The primary advantage of using a bank is continuity since banks do not die. Also a certain level of competence, professionalism and accountability can be expected from a chartered institution that is not necessarily expected from an individual.

Kennedy already was the beneficiary of trust funds established by his father. One can assume that the level of financial sophistication in the Kennedy family was such that a bank was deemed unnecessary or that other arrangements were contemplated by the executors.

MUTUAL FUNDS

Perhaps the most popular form of professional money management employed by American investors is the mutual fund. A mutual fund simply combines the assets of many investors and manages them as one portfolio. While there are numerous variations of this simple concept, the efficiencies of pooling are immediately obvious. Where an investor with $10,000 may be unable individually to buy the many different securities he feels might be appropriate for his needs, the use of one or more mutual funds will allow him to do precisely that.

Jim Riepe is president of marketing for T. Rowe Price Associates. As a parent he is very sensitive to the effect of affluence on children. He believes that the development of healthy attitudes towards money should be a goal of parenting. While agreeing that attitude development is a parental responsibility, he also believes that schools can help the learning process. To this end he and his colleagues are active in making presentations at local schools on subjects related to money and finance.

Jim also points out that 90 percent of T. Rowe Price's customers are college educated and 50 percent have advanced degrees. Certainly the higher incomes one associates with higher education levels have much to do with these statistics. However, another factor may be the somewhat indirect nature of investing in mutual funds. There is a difference between buying one hundred shares of General Motors and buying an equity fund which holds a ten thousand share position in the same company. Using mutual funds is a refinement that is learned easily. Jim suggests that a regular reading of their literature will provide a nutshell education on many typical investment and economic matters.

The main advantage of mutual funds is professional management. Regardless of whether you are buying bonds, stocks, real estate, or gold there are funds managed by experts in the field available for purchase. Another advantage to mutual funds is the custodial and accounting function. All the security and bookkeeping associated with managing a portfolio is taken care of by the fund. Finally, there is liquidity; funds can be bought and sold quite easily.

Like any investment, deciding to invest in mutual funds requires some homework. For example, there are load funds, no load funds, open end funds, and closed end funds. The important thing to remember is that the funds exist and are available if they meet your investment needs. As an example of how one might use mutual funds, let's look at what is offered by T. Rowe Price. T. Rowe Price offers the family of mutual funds listed below. Each one is professionally managed and is designed to achieve a unique investment objective.

PRIME RESERVE FUND.   The Prime Reserve Fund invests in very high quality money market securities like certificates of deposit for principal safety and yield.

U.S. TREASURY MONEY FUND.   This money fund provides an extra measure of protection by investing only in securities guaranteed by the full faith and credit of the United States government—e.g. U.S. Treasury Bills.

TAX-EXEMPT MONEY FUND.   This money fund aims for safety of principal and a competitive current income that is completely exempt from federal income taxes. It invests in bonds and other tax-free securities with maturities of less than one year.

CALIFORNIA TAX-FREE MONEY FUND.   For stability and money market income that is exempt from federal and California state income taxes, this fund invests in the highest quality short-term municipal securities issued by or on behalf of the state of California.

NEW YORK TAX-FREE BOND FUND.   Seeking high, triple tax-free income for New York taxpayers, this fund invests in higher quality, long-term municipal securities issued by or on behalf of the state of New York, or by other New York tax-exempt issuers. Its income is exempt from federal, New York State, and local income taxes.

HIGH YIELD FUND.   This fund invests aggressively in a wide range of medium- to lower-quality, longer-term bonds.

TAX-FREE HIGH YIELD FUND.   For investors seeking the highest tax-free income available, this fund invests in long-term, medium- to lower-quality municipal bonds.

INTERNATIONAL STOCK FUND.   Because foreign economic and stock market cycles tend to differ from those in the U.S., the International Stock Fund can be an excellent addition to investments based in the United States.

GROWTH STOCK FUND.   This fund invests in established, profitable companies, both at home and abroad. The portfolio focuses on industry leaders that have proven their ability to produce rising sales and earnings over a number of business cycles. The fund's primary goal is capital appreciation, with increasing future dividends as a secondary goal.

CAPITAL APPRECIATION FUND. This fund takes an aggressive approach to building capital by investing in undervalued and out-of-favor stocks, and balances its approach with prudent risk management. The fund has the flexibility to move into short-term money market investments during times of market uncertainty. Capital growth is the fund's only goal.

NEW ERA FUND. Companies that own or develop natural resources like gold, oil, chemicals, forest products, and other basic commodities are this fund's focus. New Era is designed for investors who want an inflation hedge with the potential for high capital growth.

EQUITY INCOME FUND. A conservative stock fund, which seeks current income and capital growth by investing in high quality stocks that pay well above average dividends. It is designed to put the power of compounding dividends to work.

GROWTH AND INCOME FUND. By searching out opportunities in undervalued, out-of-favor stocks, this fund aims for both capital growth and current income. It is expected to be less volatile than stocks in general.

NEW AMERICA GROWTH FUND. This fund invests in leading companies in the fastest growing part of the American economy: the service sector. The fund invests in companies in the financial services, health care, travel and leisure, food service, airline, media, and computer software industries, among others.

NEW HORIZONS FUND. This aggressive fund invests exclusively in small, rapidly growing companies. It aims to seek out companies with outstanding long-term profit potential.

SHORT-TERM BOND FUND. Designed to give a higher-than-money-market yield without the volatility of longer-term bonds.

TAX-FREE SHORT-INTERMEDIATE FUND. Investing exclusively in tax-free securities with maturities of seven years or less, this fund is for investors who want a higher-than-money-market yield with greater stability than longer-term municipal bond funds.

NEW INCOME FUND. This fund aims to provide high income over the long term and a positive total return in all markets by investing in high quality, longer-term corporate bonds and other debt securities. Management adjusts the portfolio's average maturity as interest rates change.

GNMA FUND. The GNMA Fund seeks the highest current income that is consistent with preserving capital and providing maximum credit protection. It invests in mortgage-backed securities that are 100 percent guaranteed for timely payment of principal and interest by the U.S. government. (The fund's share price and yield are not guaranteed.)

INTERNATIONAL BOND FUND. The International Bond Fund aims to provide high current income, capital growth potential, and all the benefits of diversifying a portfolio worldwide, by investing mainly in high quality bonds issued in foreign currencies.

The table below groups the funds by level of risk.

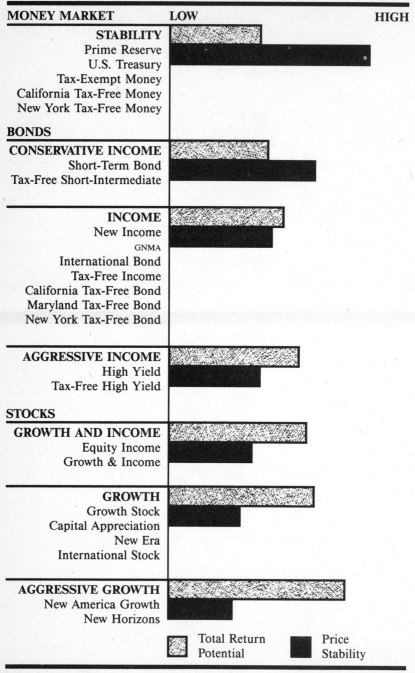

MONEY MARKET   LOW   HIGH

STABILITY
Prime Reserve
U.S. Treasury
Tax-Exempt Money
California Tax-Free Money
New York Tax-Free Money

BONDS

CONSERVATIVE INCOME
Short-Term Bond
Tax-Free Short-Intermediate

INCOME
New Income
GNMA
International Bond
Tax-Free Income
California Tax-Free Bond
Maryland Tax-Free Bond
New York Tax-Free Bond

AGGRESSIVE INCOME
High Yield
Tax-Free High Yield

STOCKS

GROWTH AND INCOME
Equity Income
Growth & Income

GROWTH
Growth Stock
Capital Appreciation
New Era
International Stock

AGGRESSIVE GROWTH
New America Growth
New Horizons

Total Return   Price
Potential   Stability

Source: T. Rowe Price.

So sophisticated is the T. Rowe Price network of funds that you can get daily quotes on the value of your funds and switch from one fund to another over the telephone.

INVOLVING CHILDREN IN SAVINGS AND INVESTMENTS

My talks with parents on the subject of savings indicate a consensus that children should open a passbook savings account fairly early in life, say at seven or eight years of age. Birthday gifts from grandparents and relatives might be the initial source of funds. A number of lessons can be learned from this practice. The idea of compound interest may well be the most important one. Certainly the discipline of saving should be initiated in the process.

Parents also can learn something about their children by observing their attitudes towards money and savings. For reasons I cannot explain children raised in the same environment will sometimes have completely different attitudes toward money and savings. I have even known twins who exhibit diametrically opposed attitudes towards money. I am sure that psychologists have explanations for this phenomenon. But for the parent, the knowledge that one child is a spendthrift and the other a compulsive saver is enough to help guide and educate them in the use of money.

Some parents have encouraged their children to purchase common stocks for the purpose of educating them in this more sophisticated form of savings. Having purchased the stock the children can monitor its fluctuation in the newspaper and receive the dividend check in the mail. The annual report will also arrive and can be read to enhance understanding of "their" company. The stock selected for this purpose is usually one whose products have high visibility, like Procter & Gamble, and with which the child can identify quickly.

Perhaps more a sign of the times than anything else is the money management camp for kids supported by Shearson Lehman Brothers in Florida. Campers are taught to read a balance sheet, the *Wall Street Journal* and manage a $100 portfolio. This may be the extreme example of how to teach your kids about money, but Smart Services, Inc. who runs the camp, has increased the number of classes from one to four over the past year.

ACTIVITIES

1. If your child expresses interest in what a particular financial institution does, use it as an opportunity to write for information and discuss the products and services. The American Banking Association Sponsors the Personal Economics Program (PEP), a national volunteer public education program of bankers who work with teachers to teach young people about "banks, banking services and personal financial management skills." This program can teach children how to be good consumers, how to balance a checkbook, use credit wisely, and budget their money. For further information, call or write:

   Personal Economics Program
   American Bankers Association
   1120 Connecticut Avenue, N.W.
   Washington, D.C. 20036
   (202) 663-5425

Part III

Money and the Future

Abraham Lincoln confirmed in his "Gettysburg Address" that America is dedicated to the proposition that all men are created equal. Nevertheless, the inequities between citizens are apparent. Equality may well be a legitimate national goal but it has not been achieved as yet.

The following chapters are designed to help parents examine their own financial situation and the economic reasons for it. I hope the insights gleaned from these thoughts can be imparted to your children to help them understand the world they live in. With these economic bearings children can develop realistic personal goals and steps they can take to increase the probability of achieving them.

Most people can look back on their lives and identify squandered opportunities in education and jobs. We all want our children to benefit from our mistakes, and exploit the opportunities which life allows.

8

The Importance of Education

"Dad, why do I have to go to school?"

There are factors other than the ecomomy which will affect your child's level of income and standard of living. Education, talent, personal choice, and to a larger degree than we want to admit, luck and circumstance. Humans, and Americans especially, do not like the idea of living in a world left to chance. We prefer our universe ordered and predictable. Science has freed us from ancient mythologies. Given our methods of analysis and technology, we can measure and predict almost anything. However comforting this thought may be, it simply is not true. The outcome of some phenomena and human activities cannot be predicted. Quantum physicists have learned that at the subatomic level the theories of Newton and Einstein no longer apply. They have come to depend on theories of probability to predict events. Much the same approach must be taken in personal career development.

The American mythology is that the great man or woman will take the reins of fate and break it to his or her will. The careers of great men and women are forever analyzed for personal traits that led to their success. Lincoln's and Washington's virtues of honesty and intellectual vigor are constantly offered to children as models of behavior with promises of similar reward. Whether it's Lee Iacocca or Admiral Rickover, every industry, profession, business or organization will have its heroes who are credited with special qualities to justify their privileges and positions. Often these individuals will themselves believe their success is a direct result of their special shrewdness and perception rather than luck and circumstance. Children, especially, will associate the individual with his level of success. How many children, when inspired by a movie hero, a teacher or even a family member, will attempt to mold themselves into that person's image only to be disillusioned by the outcome. Probability allows for enough success stories to keep each generation going, but one cannot help but believe that the predictable disappointment of the many outweighs the success of a few. The question is, how can it be otherwise? And the answer is knowledge.

SUCCESS AND CHANCE

Children can be taught to admire not only individuals and their virtues, but also to understand the political ideas and economic forces that affect their times and dictate to us all. Children should consider that life may not be a basket of goodies to pick from, but more like a fast-moving river that can be navigated only by our wits and the circumstances we encounter. Children should also consider that their decision tools as navigator will not be the simple logic of cause and effect, but the relentless application of probability. Children so taught will be more in touch with reality and not in the ethereal realm of dreams. They will anticipate failure earlier, and make decisions consistent with the world around them. This power of prediction will lessen their confusion and add to their personal happiness and appreciation of life.

Let us try an analogy. Say your son sees the movie *Top Gun* and decides he wants to be a Navy fighter pilot. What should be his mental approach. With the wonderful enthusiasm of youth he will have few doubts as to his success. Never mind that thousands of other young men with whom he must compete will have been similarly inspired, he alone will prevail. As a parent, however, you can immediately see the shoals in the river he has decided to enter. Look back at any class of Navy pilots and you will see a vast sea of might-have-beens. Coming out of that movie in the summer of 1986 thousands of young men and women looked up and dreamed of racing across the sky in awesomely powered machines. But what will happen? Some will flunk out of high school or college. Many will have physical problems. Eyes will fail. Drugs will dominate or distort some lives. Girls will become pregnant. Auto crashes will maim and destroy. Some for reasons never explained, will simply not be selected. The son of a senator or an admiral will be pushed forward over equally qualified peers. Or a Naval Academy graduate will be given the edge over his contemporary from Purdue. Others will change their minds because of another experience or person.

The point is that the probability of any one individual achieving a particular job or position is fairly remote. But the probabilities change rapidly given certain events. Take our fighter pilot for example. If your son is an "A" student with superior athletic ability his chances improve remarkably. If he chooses to go to the Naval Academy, they get even better. If his father happens to be an admiral who was also a fighter pilot it begins to look like a sure thing. Nevertheless, when our mythical fighter pilot class is formed there will be members who by all odds should not be there. That is because there is a certain randomness to life, and of such stuff are dreams and hopes made.

What does this mean to the parent? Should he discourage his son from becoming a fighter pilot? Absolutely not. But the child should be aware of the odds he faces. He also should be aware of his strengths and use them to his best advantage. Ultimately, this self knowledge of his strengths and weaknesses should lead the child into a career choice where the probabilities of success are the highest.

"HOW MUCH MONEY WILL I MAKE?"

Most people do not like to focus on probabilities because that smacks of predestination and the loss of free will. They prefer to focus on the real but improbable extremes. Nevertheless, at any point in time our future earnings and associated standard of living are fairly predictable. In the case of the very rich and the very poor we accept this almost instinctively. That the rich will remain rich and get richer is a motivating factor in American life. If you can get it, you will be able to keep it and pass it on to your heirs.

Trend in Concentration Of Income

Percentage of total family income

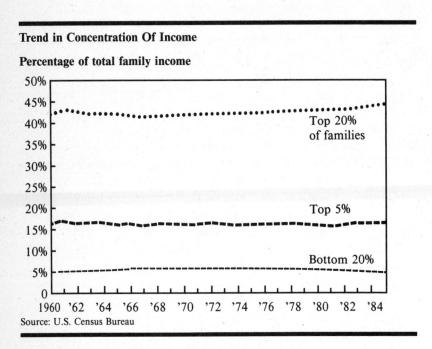

Source: U.S. Census Bureau

The literary and broadcast media pander to our desire to focus on the improbable extreme. A favorite theme of literature is the overcoming of adversity to achieve success. Scarlet O'Hara, clutching the earth of Tara and crying that she will never go hungry again, makes for a great movie. The reality was much different. Most Southerners were crushed by the Civil War. The work of generations was wiped out. The Southern economy did not recover for a hundred years, and the region's standard of living was well below the national average for decades.

At the other extreme, John Steinbeck's *The Grapes of Wrath* has been praised for its stark reality because he took the poor and made them poorer. This was a fair assessment because depressions do precisely that. But his description was extreme. Had the majority of Americans suffered as much as the mythical Joads, the American experiment would probably have ended in a bloody revolution. That it did not is an accolade to the resilience of American democracy.

Children should not dwell on the extremes of the economic spectrum unless of course they happen to be there already. They should focus on the probable course of their lives given their personal circumstances. If they are ever going to exploit the future, they must have expectations consistent with their circumstances. If they have been favored by circumstance they should know and understand it. If they have not been favored they should know that as well. It is equally important to the happiness of the rich and poor child alike that each understands the consequences of his economic condition. Reality focuses the mind. Illusion breeds disillusionment.

In his Pulitzer Prize winning *Common Ground*, Anthony Lukas describes an argument between working-class black parents and middle-class white parents over the curriculum at their local primary school. The gist of the debate centers on whether the class should be highly structured or more open. The wise conclusion of the working class parents was that "an emphasis on personal choice was fine for children with a lifetime of choices ahead of them, but not for the poor, who would need discipline to prevail over life's rigors." To carry the thought a little further one could describe the difference among being poor, middle class, or rich, as the range of choices one has regarding his life. The wealthier the person, the greater his flexibility in choosing a course in life.

Nevertheless, many parents never present their children with the choices their relative income affords. For Americans who have evolved from the harshness of Ellis Island, the frontier, and the Depression, there is simply never enough money. Work and accumulating wealth are the sole choices in life. Only some mythical millionaire ever has enough that he need not worry. The insecurity wrought by the harshness of the American environment pervades our national psyche. Parents continue to foster in their children an economic insecurity that drives them into the marketplace with a compulsion that can never be satisfied.

This unsatisfied compulsion and resulting anxiety is only half of the unhappiness equation. Someone said that the sadness of life is not what is, but what might have been. Americans pursue wealth, and even if successful, are robbed of the time to appreciate their more fulfilling talents.

The choice of career and how to finance it should begin early and preferably with enlightened parental guidance. The expected income return
from most careers and professions is highly predictable, and closely associated with one's level of education. The following table demon-
strates the correlation between education and income.

Household Income	All Households	College Graduate Households
Under $10,000	21.1%	5.9%
$10,000 - 14,999	12.2	6.0
$15,000 - 19,999	11.4	7.8
$20,000 - 24,999	10.4	8.6
$25,000 - 34,999	16.9	18.0
$35,000 - 49,999	15.3	22.5
$50,000 - 74,999	9.0	19.5
$75,000 and over	3.7	11.7

Source: Reprinted with permission, Copyright *American Demographics* 1987

There are extremes in every industry but the probability of achieving these levels is low and depends in most cases on factors beyond one's
control. If, for example, your child desires a career in medical or health
services, the first determinant of his success will be his education. High
school diplomas, and undergraduate degrees, master's and doctoral degrees will all command different salary levels. A child should know this.
If the possibility of college and advanced degrees is limited by family
circumstances, a plan for continuing education should be a factor in selecting an employer. Will the employer provide the time and money for
furthering the educational aspirations of its employees?

The next question to ask is what the income expectations are for various jobs in the industry. Often management will be the highest paid,
but not always. Individual salesman in every industry often top the salaries of all but the highest manager. Marketing is a crucial segment of
business and is usually well compensated. A person may find that call-
ing on doctors and dentists is more enjoyable and rewarding than a nine
to five office job executing company policy. If one is strictly a technician operating a lab or testing service, the attraction may be found in
more flexible work hours or independence, even if at somewhat re-

duced earnings. Management career patterns also should be analyzed. Are the managers brought in from outside or promoted from within? Do they come from sales, staff or elsewhere.

Again, the point to be emphasized is knowledge of self and realistic expectations for one's chosen career. A high school graduate who decides to be a lab technician should realize the limited monetary potential and adjust to it early in life. Or the college graduate who begins as a management trainee for a major corporation should be aware of the probability of where she will end up and why.

The best source of this self-knowledge is the parent. No one else has observed the child more closely. No one is more aware of her strengths and weaknesses. It is we parents who must guide, support and reinforce our children in developing their talents and aspirations. While this may sound like common sense, and it is, many of us don't pursue it when raising our children. A favorite Hollywood scene is the father, peering at his newborn son, extolling a litany of achievement he has planned for him. Star football player, president of the family company, attendance at dad's college, are always high on the list. Not only are dad's expectations unrealistic, he perpetuates the problem by establishing standards for the son that may be totally inappropriate. Our unwillingness to accept the randomness of life or our inability to accept our lack of control initiates a cycle of disappointment. In a way we set ourselves up by pinning our happiness to an unpredictable outcome.

Let us say a young woman decides to be a pharmacist. Obviously if her father is a pharmacist things look pretty good for her. If she is a bright student and gains acceptance to a good school things are even better. If she has an independent source of income that will allow her to take additional or advanced degrees, she is in truly fortunate circumstances. But what if none of these things applies? Suppose she comes from a family of six with one low wage earner supporting the whole bunch. She may have to take the minimum baccalaureate degree in pharmacy and go right to work. It is unlikely that she could go into business for herself. She might go with a chain and step into a managerial position. Maybe she will go to work for a drug company as a salesman or in a supervising position in the manufacturing of drugs. The field is broad and rich with potential. The rewards are many but what about the money? In 1984 the average pharmacist earned about $30,000 year. Ten percent earned above $42,000 and 10 percent earned less than $16,000. Let us diagram it.

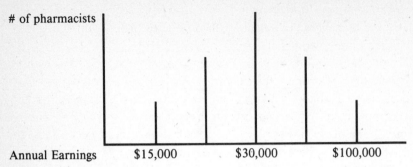

# of pharmacists

Annual Earnings $15,000 $30,000 $100,000

Source: U.S. Census Bureau

Someplace way over to the right of our chart are graduates of pharmacy colleges who make more than $100,000 a year. Usually they will be the recipients of favorable circumstances such as those described above, circumstances over which they had little control. Yes, they worked hard and applied themselves. So too did some of the people to the far left of our chart who make $15,000. However, in the latter cases personal circumstances and a little less luck (like personal illness) diminished their earning power. You will note, however, for the vast majority the expected salary return was around $30,000. This was well above the national average of $21,000, and on a par with a number of other high paying industries such as communications and mining.

HOW IMPORTANT IS MONEY?

I once had a very talented friend who said, "Happiness is doing your own thing and making a buck at it." On the surface his statement seemed to say that in America a certain amount of money is necessary for a happy life, which is true. But one must also fulfill his own talents and destiny. However, he made this statement in answer to a question asking why he had decided to attend Harvard Business School. The implication of his answer was that the Harvard MBA would insure that he made money regardless of his chosen field. Well, I don't know what he learned at Harvard, but success in one's chosen field cannot be absolutely predetermined. Certainly by going to Harvard Business School my friend enhanced his chances for monetary success because a high quality education usually does. Nevertheless, his actual income would depend on his chosen field and the external economic factors that would come to bear in that industry during his period of involvement. As it turned out, he wrongly decided that money and happiness were pretty much synonymous and separated his self-fulfillment, or doing his own thing, from making money. To date he is quite wealthy but not particularly fulfilled. He has a nagging suspicion that the acquisition of wealth has precluded the development of his more creative talents. However, he is young and perhaps can yet step away from money making to do other things.

Someplace along the line my friend could have had a burst of insight that would have allowed him to develop his finer talents. Ideally that some place would have been his parents' home. This burst of insight was somewhat unlikely because his parents themselves were insecure and felt a need to acquire wealth. The children of immigrants, they knew and feared poverty. One should prepare for the worst and so they instructed their son. I would be the last to belittle concerns about financial security given America's economic history. Still there is a limit as to what can be done. To a great degree our fate is entwined with our fellow humans. The individual must strive to develop his own resources and talents virtually independent, but fully aware, of the economic circumstances surrounding his life. One should not pursue wealth to be happy, but rather be happy with the wealth one has.

One might conclude from what I have written that the wealthy are in the best position of all. I would agree that they should be, but the truth is that this is not always so. Independent wealth provides an underpinning for personal happiness but it certainly doesn't guarantee it. Wealth is relative, especially among the rich. Someone fairly well off can easily conclude they are relatively poor and be miserable as a result. The rich have their own problems when it comes to income and supporting a lifestyle. A common problem is the diminishment of the family fortune as it is split up among the children.

THE PROBLEMS OF THE RICH

I once knew a man who had several million dollars, which provided a nice income of $160,000 a year with an equivalent standard of living. He inherited the money from a grandfather who had made a bundle during the twenties. His personal calling was to the foreign service where he was modestly successful but, as you would suspect, added nothing to the family fortune. When he died, his children, of which there were four, each received $300,000 in trust after the payment of estate taxes. The income from each trust was estimated at $18,000 a year. It readily became apparent to each child that the schools they attended and the country clubs they played in would not automatically accrue to their own children. And they would have to work for a living. Unfortunately, they had not been well prepared for this highly predictable state of affairs. Like tigers in a zoo their competitive instincts had been dulled by their comfortable surroundings. While well educated they could not expect earnings that much greater than their peers'. The extent to which they had higher expectations was due to their social contacts and relatives. The children always gave off an air of unfulfilled expectations, as if they should be living better than they were. The bank directorships, the business deals, the charity trusteeships that were rightfully theirs, somehow had slipped away. But in truth these things were never likely to be. Those coveted positions in fact went to a local businessman, who got in the way of a major construction boom and realized profits beyond his wildest dreams.

Although well off by several measures, the children never benefited because their parents never prepared them for the reality of their circumstances. Because of their privileged upbringing, their expectations were so high that they were sure to be disappointed. Had their father or mother enhanced the family fortune, then perhaps these expectations would have been realized. But this was not the case. Given the father's chosen profession and restricted income the children should have lowered their expectations, and developed their own talents within the highly predictable financial circumstances in which they found themselves.

Another family I knew handled the situation quite differently. Heir to a $7 million publishing fortune the family was headed by a widowed mother and consisted of six married children and numerous grandchildren. Each Christmas the matriarch would gather all the children around the dining room table and review the family financial situation. There was no pretense of equality. Those who were in need received more than those who were not. Educational talent was rewarded with scholarships and less endowed children were compensated in other ways. The family with six children received more than the family with none. While there was no pretense of equality there was none at secrecy either. Each meeting was attended by lawyers who explained wills and trust provisions so that all knew what distributions would take place and when. If trusts were established, the designated trustees were named and the trust provisions detailed. Each child knew exactly what he would get and when. Also in attendance were bankers and investment advisors so that portfolios could be reviewed and questions answered. Income projections and risk levels were also discussed so that probabilities concerning future distributions could be assessed.

These procedures created a healthy state of family affairs. No one was kept in the dark about what to expect. When the matriarch died, the tradition continued under slightly different circumstances but the openess continued. The animosity and resentment generated by secrecy was kept at bay and the family enjoyed their good fortune to the greatest extent possible.

Under such circumstances each child could judge for himself the standard of living he desired and to what extent the family's wealth would support it. One son became a lawyer whose earned income more than matched the $50,000 of annual income eventually allocated to him under the family's trust. Another son pursued a career in music and for the most part relied on the trust's income for a modest standard of living. While their life styles and standards of living were quite different, both brothers appeared satisfied because their expectations never exceeded actual circumstances. While the circumstances and numbers will be different, the same objective and unemotional approach to family income is appropriate for us less fortunate people as well.

THE PROBLEMS OF THE POOR

The marketing media is fond of using stars of whatever variety to promote their sponsor's products. Not surprisingly the same technique is used to promote other activities as well. Children are exposed constantly to successful entertainers from the world of sports or the cinema expressing virtues with the implication that their success is somehow related. Such expressions trigger unrealistic dreams that distract the disadvantaged child from the reality of his life. Game shows, the lottery, and the like are all visual drugs that numb the child to the harshness of his destiny with false hopes of any easy reprieve from the labor that will be his lot. All men may be created equal under the law but the odds are stacked against the poor. Involvement in drugs, single parent homes, incomplete educations, limited income and opportunities, all conspire to limit success. Under such circumstances, it is not surprising that a young man would escape into dreams of playing in the NBA for big bucks. But it is a false hope. The probability of financial success is extremely low. Unfortunately our heritage, skin color and the attitudes of our fellow citizens are not things over which we have much individual control. We cannot change society but we can change ourselves. This flexibility allows us to exploit our opportunities, limited as they might be. Statistically the obvious steps are to finish high school with good grades, get a college scholarship if possible, build a strong marriage, stay away from drugs, and pursue steady employment. Some would say that financial success fosters stronger homes, better education records and health habits. This may be true. Human behavior patterns are mainly self-reinforcing. The question is, where does the cycle begin? The answer has to be in the mind of the individual. Proper thoughts lead to proper actions, which will slowly shift the probability of success to our favor.

For any of this economic evolution to take place, opportunity must exist. The American economic system, if it has done nothing else, has provided opportunity. If the proverbial man from Mars came to earth and asked which nation provides the greatest opportunity for making money he would have to be told America. America provides jobs and opportunity to a fault. We have polluted our environment, corrupted our governments, and strained our financial system, all in the name of jobs and opportunity. Jobs have been the promise of American democracy and for the most part that promise has been delivered. Belief in job opportunity must not be a false hope if democracy is to succeed. But equally important are the individual and cultural attitudes of the work force. Any businessman will tell you that good workers are hard to find. A highly motivated worker will pay for herself. Does that mean that if you work hard you will succeed? No, life is full of traps. No amount of hard work can prevent being laid off if external economic forces dictate a cutback in the labor force. The reality of lay-offs does not mitigate the value of hard work, it simply confirms the uncertainty of any job.

Even though the odds may be stacked against the poor, opportunities will arise. If a child is made to confront the reality of his circumstances, he will be more inclined to exploit the opportunities he has. If you were to tell a child he had a disease that probably would leave him crippled if left alone but that a certain treatment, albeit painful, would increase his chances of a normal life to 50/50, what course do you think he would choose? Even if there was a slim chance that he would recover without treatment, most parents and children would choose to increase the odds. After all, why not? Yet when faced with similar circumstances regarding a crippled standard of living, children let slip the opportunity of education, to shift the odds against their fate. The reason is often that parents and teachers have failed to teach their children the economic facts of life.

ACTIVITIES

1. Review the U.S. Department of Labor Statistics' *Occupational Outlook Handbook* with your child. It is a very useful source of information about what jobs will be paying in the future to help your child understand how her career choice—and the education she will need to achieve it—will affect her life style. This book is available from the Superintendent of Documents, U.S. Government Printing Office, Washington, D.C. 20402.

2. Many, many books have been published on helping your child make a good career choice. Check some of these books out of your local library and help your child explore the world of work. Encourage him to talk to adults who are working in the fields in which he is interested.

9

Making It in America Tomorrow

"When I grow up, I want to be a fireman."

When I was growing up back in the sixties, it readily became apparent that the two primary sources of American post-adolescent anxiety were sex and money. These anxieties grew from a secrecy imparted by parents who were equally confused and unsure about these emotional subjects. We resolved the sexual problem by throwing convention to the wind and rewriting the American code of sexual ethics. Through experimentation and analysis, we taught ourselves what our parents had failed to. But with money the approach was a little different.

As we matured we accepted the reality that standard of living is based for the most part upon income. To be sure, standard of living is not the same as quality of life, but to a degree they are interrelated. The best things in life are free, but in America food, shelter, clothing, education, and vacations cost money. Now as parents we constantly grapple with the problem of income and standard of living, and as adults most of us handle it fairly well. With a combination of hard work, instinct, and acceptance, we carve out a spot on the American economic landscape and settle in, or in a word, we cope. As with other aspects of the life cycle, these experiments will be passed on to our children and here is where the problems will start.

TEACHING OUR CHILDREN ABOUT MONEY

The transfer of knowledge between parent and child is a fascinating subject. Cultural anthropologists have traced behavior patterns back generations. Techniques of child-rearing have passed from mother to daughter virtually unchanged for hundreds of years. In a stable environment there is a certain evolutionary consistency to this process. However, when the environment changes, the techniques of one generation become worthless and irrelevant to the next. For this reason certain facts of life need to be revised before being passed down to the next generation. Sometimes these facts can be organized into a curriculum of study and taught through institutions like schools. Some subjects, however, are so personal that formal instruction is deemed inappropriate. Certainly sexual behavior, religion, and politics fall into this category. For example, primary and secondary schools are allowed to instruct students in the organization of our government, but generally they will not advocate a liberal or conservative bias. For much the same reasons economics and finance are not taught in our elementary schools. The highly politicized nature of our economy makes it unsuitable for schools. Or put another way, the study of economics has not resulted in truths so widely accepted that they can be put forth in formal education. As a consequence, parents are left with the responsibility of instructing their children on the economic realities of life. For the most part parents will fall back on their own narrow experience, and the attitudes learned from their parents.

OUTSIDE INFLUENCES

Some say that the truths of our economy are, in fact, well known by the high priests of Wall Street, and the members of the Federal Reserve

Board who use their knowledge to manipulate the economy and society. While events sometimes may seem to confirm this belief, the reality is somewhat simpler. Our economy is designed to serve our society and provide the most good for the most people by promoting justice and political stability. And design may be too strong a word because it implies a greater amount of control than actually exists. The American system is a free market system that allows individuals and institutions to decide how their incomes are to be earned, invested, and spent. A free market is defined as individuals coming together to exchange goods and services at an agreed upon price. The mystery of the market is that all these individual decisions in combination create an independent force that in turn affects individual decisions, somewhat like a chemical reaction. For example, the purchase of an automobile is an independent decision of each consumer. But so great is the combined impact of these many independent decisions that the health of the economy is often measured by them. If consumers decide to buy autos in large numbers, the effect ripples through the economy affecting many industries unrelated to automobiles themselves. The questions prompted by this example are obvious. Does a healthy economy promote a lot of car buying or does a lot of car buying promote a healthy economy? If the latter is true, where does the consumer get the money to make his purchase? These are precisely the questions that policy makers must address and resolve. As they mature, children should develop an awareness of this process and its effect on their lives.

THE FREE MARKET SYSTEM

In a sense, the free market makes certain decisions for you. The market determines which occupations will receive what income, which investments are sound, and what products can be purchased. But it does this through a market mechanism, not by the laws or edicts of an individual or group. From time to time the government does insert itself into the economy to achieve limited political objectives. These forays are normally short-lived because they often cause distortions or unfair advantage. The fallback position is always the market.

The American economy is the most dynamic in the world. Like a living machine it lurches through history tackling one job after another and using each step as a springboard for the next. It might be quite fascinating to the disinterested observer, but since we live here we cannot enjoy such a detached viewpoint. Each American, as a duty of citizenship and self-survival, should have a good feel for the direction, dangers, and goals of our economic policy.

To illustrate a bit, let us draw an analogy. In a war everyone knows that the infantry and fighter pilots will take the heat. They are psychologically puffed up and given some ribbons to mask their gruesome fate. Likewise, everyone knows that the quartermaster will have a less hazardous job, and while he won't win any ribbons, his life expectancy will be much greater. But in 1980 when Paul Volcker, then chairman of the Federal Reserve Board, set out to crush inflation there was no such designation. The farmer, the miner, the oil worker were to become the infantry of the inflation war. But there was no psychological preparation for their fate. Perhaps it is unrealistic to expect politicians and other leaders to dwell on the negative aspects of their decisions, but since they won't, who will? In fairness some provisions were made to take the sting out of the deflation, but these provisions were designed to protect our financial system and not necessarily to relieve the pain of any group or individual. Unless an individual farmer or miner could sense the impending economic tide, and prepare himself and his family, the disaster looming on the horizon might well have engulfed him. To one degree or another the same economic forces, guided by policy makers, will affect each one of us by enhancing or diminishing our income and standard of living.

WHY TEACH CHILDREN ABOUT THE ECONOMY

Developing a child's awareness of the economy is not to make her rich but rather to make her happy. Economic knowledge and predictability lead to decision or acceptance, either one of which will normally lessen the anxiety associated with the unknown. Take our farmer, for example, who wisely predicted the deflationary cycle that hit our economy in 1980. Should he have forgone being a farmer and become a stockbroker? Heaven's no! After all, a man has to do what he has to do. But certainly he would not have mortgaged the farm with the idea that even higher commodity prices would generate the income to pay off his loans. On the contrary, he would have restructured his operation to lower his cash needs and thereby lessen the impact of his reduced income. If our farmer had been the son of a farmer who had prospered during the inflation-ridden seventies, he might well have thought the game would go on forever. The local John Deere tractor salesman undoubtedly would have filled his head with stories of worldwide food shortages, and the Russians' unending lust for grain. This unprepared youngster might well have decided to expand the family operation at precisely the moment the Federal Reserve was cranking up its first salvo against inflation. In retrospect it seems obvious, but it wasn't then. Anyone who had suggested for example, that oil would fall from $37 to $10 a barrel in five years would have been laughed at. Price deflation simply was not something that recent experience made plausible. Nevertheless, five years later in 1985 we had Willie Nelson staging concerts to raise money for the destitute farmer who lost his land because he could not operate it on the money people were willing to pay him for his crop. Knowledge would not have made the farmer rich, but it would have allowed him to survive.

Economic knowledge in this sense has a direct application to a person's well-being. But what about the other children nestled in suburbia? Where does this knowledge fit in? Well, for one thing it explains things. It gives them the answers to the questions underlying the evening news stories. To virtually every human action or decision there is an economic linchpin, which if removed will tumble the entire endeavor. This is not cynicism; this is reality. Earth is a hostile environment in which man must constantly struggle if he is to survive. As parents we should imbue our children with an understanding of the economic fabric that underlies all human endeavor. It will add a dimension to their thinking process.

Children, by experience and education, are taught to analyze by developing cause and effect relationships. If they see a building going up, they view it in terms of men putting material together to construct an office for someone to use. The idea that the building is being erected primarily to create jobs for the builders is a simple abstraction they normally would not consider. Children are brought up in a very utilitarian and practical world. There is a direct reason and rationale for everything. My daughter is particularly adept at asking a question and following up every answer with a "why?" It can be fun for about three minutes and then my limited reasons for doing things begin to show. For example, try to explain why you wear a tie to work. Because everybody else does? To keep my neck warm? There is probably a good sociological reason I wear a tie, but when it comes to fashion I think like a child and can construe no practical reason for it. If I shift gears to my economic mode, I immediately see the vast profits to be made by wrapping expensive pieces of cloth around men's necks, directly in front of their mouths, thereby necessitating frequent replacement. But how did they get us to do it? Is there a powerful tie maker's union some place that supplies free ties to socially prominent individuals like Tom Brokaw, which then requires the rest of us to go out and buy the worthless things? It's a mystery worthy of someone's doctoral dissertation I am sure.

THE PARENTAL EXPERIENCE

When children become aware of gaps in their economic thinking, they pursue the truth with questions. But all too often, rather than getting thoughtful answers they are taught the unexamined experiences of the parent. One example might be the son of the steelworker who has listened for years to his father's praise of the union. "Get in the union and they'll take care of you." Steelworkers make steel and struggle with the bad guys at management to wrest their fair share. That is the lore, the tradition. The stories of bloody riots to win precious rights are fresh in the parent's memory. They are passed on to the son as if they were a craft developed over the ages. There is, to be sure, a dim awareness that the Japanese are building more efficient plants, with American money yet. But would Americans give money to the Japanese to build plants that will eliminate American jobs? Hell no! The Union would never allow that. Can they stop it? Damn right they can! The child gets into the union but events overtake him. Steel prices fall, American plants close. The job is lost. The anxiety and trauma take their toll.

The story does not always end the same way. Some children follow in their parents' footsteps and use that base to achieve more than the parent. In fact most modern American success stories are at least two generations in the making. Whether it is a law practice, a construction business, or even a political career, the ground work is often laid by one generation and built upon by the next. There is something called the mentor connection which cannot be denied. Men since ancient times have groomed protégés to inherit their power and connections. Often it is a son. But within a highly structured bureaucracy, like a major corporation or government institution, bright young executives will be singled out for promotion and advancement. Nor does the mentor-protégé relationship have to be a personal one. A good executive can evaluate and monitor the advancement of young managers whose style she admires, without a close or social relationship. The point is that many are called but few are chosen, and the process of choosing may involve bias depending on the personalities involved.

For example, a recent survey of the one hundred richest people in Washington indicated that more than seventy-five percent were associated with a family concern, the beneficiary of an inheritance, or the product of a well connected family. Nor should one expect it to be otherwise. People tend to favor their families and those they love. The right to leave your children the product of your labor is seen as a basic American right and is recognized as so by our laws. Another somewhat more subtle factor is time. Sometimes an asset like land, a small business, or even a law practice will lie dormant for generations until economic forces come to bear and create a fortune almost overnight.

Does this mentor factor or generation building mean anything for your child? Should he or she go running about looking for someone's coattails to latch on to? No, I do not think so. I think one should only realize that it exists. If one is so fortunate, if that is the right word, to be selected for special consideration she should go into the relationship with her eyes wide open. And if one finds himself without a mentor, he should realize that his prospects may be diminished as a result. There are many other factors to evaluate when one considers his prospects, but in many organizations or professions the absence of a mentor overseeing one's development, can be important. Likewise, one should appreciate the advantage of inheriting a family business or going into business with a well established parent.

There is a less attractive aspect of special mentor relationships. Being the boss's son, marrying the boss's daughters, or simply being perceived as an apple polisher are all somewhat pejorative descriptions. It is difficult to be one of the boys and at the same time not share in their frustrations because one has been singled out for special consideration.

CONCLUSION

The need to educate our children in matters of money and finance presents parents with a responsibility and an opportunity. The responsibility I hope has been made clear in the preceeding pages. Every well raised child is taught certain basic rules of personal health; bathe daily, brush your teeth, see your doctor and dentist on a regular basis. The absence of these habits is an immediate sign of neglect. Lack of knowledge of personal finance soon will be viewed the same way. The child uneducated in these basics will be less able to negotiate the pitfalls of our society. Those better aware of financial and economic matters will have a better understanding of the workings of our society and be more secure as a result.

Parents and schools are also presented an opportunity in providing this instruction. So pervasive are money decisions in our society that we can use them as a substitute training ground for developing our children's decision making instincts. Quantification, evaluation, trading off, are all thought processes that adults and organizations go through constantly in the course of their daily lives. Children are naturally sheltered from the process until they leave home, at which time it falls on them like a ton of bricks. It is no wonder so many have difficulty. Unwise career choices, and financial problems are often the result. With a little time and common sense parents can make it otherwise.

Suggested Reading
For You and Your
Children

Belliston, Larry. *Extra Cash for Kids.* Cincinnati: Writer's Digest
Books, 1982.
- moneymaking projects for 8–10 year olds.

Berenstain, Stan. *The Berenstain Bears' Trouble with Money.* New
York: Random House, 1983.
- moneymaking projects for 6–8 year olds

Buehr, Walter. *Treasure—The Story of Money and Its Safeguarding.*
New York: G.P. Putnam, 1955.
- how money is printed

Byers, Patricia. *The Kids' Money Book: Great Money Making Ideas.*
Cockeysville, MD: Liberty Publishing, 1983.
- moneymaking projects for 8–12 year olds

Cohen, Daniel. *Gold: The Fascinating Story of the Noble Metal through the Ages.* New York: M. Evans, 1976.
● the history of gold

Colen, Dan. *The Money Movers: What Banks Do and Why.* New York: McKay, 1978.
● all about banking

Cooke, David Coxe. *How Money Is Made.* New York: Dodd, 1972.
● how money is printed

Custom Comic Services. *Meet the Bank.* Austin, TX: Custom Comic Services, 1988. (Distributed by the American Bankers Association Personal Economics Program)
● a child's journey through the banking system.

Federal Reserve Bank of New York. *The Story of Checks and Electronic Payments.* New York, NY: Federal Reserve Bank of New York, 1979.
● what happens to your check after you've written it.

Fitzgibbon, Dan. *All about Your Money.* New York: Antheneum, 1984.
● personal finance for kids

Forman, Brenda. *America's Place in the World Economy.* San Diego: Harcourt Brace Jovanovich Inc., 1969.
● economics

Friedman, D.H. and Parnow, C.J. *The Story of Money.* New York, NY: Federal Reserve Bank of New York, 1984.
● the history of money and how it works

Future Homemakers of America. *Financial Fitness Handbook.* Reston, VA: Future Homemakers of America, Inc., 1987
● A teen peer education program sponsored by *Changing Times.*

Haldane, Bernard. *The New Young People's Guide to Job Power.* Washington, D.C.: Acropolis Books, 1976.
● job-finding guide for teens

Hobson, Burton. *Coin Collecting as a Hobby.* New York: Sterling, 1982.
- how to collect coins

Hummel, Dean L. and McDaniel, Carl. *Unlock Your Child's Potential.* Washington, D.C.: Acropolis Books, 1979.
- how to help your child plan a career

James, Elizabeth. *Managing Your Money.* Milwaukee: Raintree, 1977.
- personal finance for kids

Kahn, Charles H. *Money Makes Sense.* Fearon, 1972.
- arithmetic, personal finance, includes teacher's manual

Kahn, Charles. *Working Makes Sense.* Fearon, 1973.
- career planning, personal finance

Leasure, Jan. *Big Bucks for Kids.* Kansas City: Andrews and McMeel, 1983.
- moneymaking projects

Martin, John. *Once Upon a Dime.* New York, NY: Federal Reserve Bank of New York.
- a fictional account of how money systems develop.

Parnow, C.J. *The Story of Consumer Credit.* New York, NY: Federal Reserve Bank of New York, 1981
- how credit affects daily lives.

Parnow, C.J. *The Story of Inflation.* New York, NY: Federal Reserve Bank of New York.
- how inflation affects daily lives.

Stenmark, Jean Kerr. *Family Math.* Oak Lawn, IL: Creative Publications.
- hundreds of family activities for every grade level, some on time and money.

Van Leuwen, Jean. *Benjy in Business.* New York: Books for Young Readers, 1983.
- basic economics for babies

Wenzel, Al. *The Story of Banks and Thrifts.* New York, NY: Federal Reserve Bank of New York.
- all about banks.

Wenzel, Al. *The Story of Foreign Trade and Exchange.* New York, NY: Federal Reserve Bank of New York.
- international trade and how it works.

Glossary of Financial Terms

The next time your child asks you a technical question about money, here are the terms you need for your answer. You can even tell your older child to "look it up," and give him this glossary to begin his research. Excerpted with permission from *A Glossary of Fiduciary Terms*, published by American Bankers Association, 1120 Connecticut Avenue, N.W., Washington, D.C. 20036, 1968, and from *Investment Companies, 47th Annual Edition*, published by Wiesenberger Investment Companies Service, One Penn Plaza, New York, New York, 10119, 1987.

Amortization—The process, in connection with bonds purchased at a premium, by which a part of the income is set aside as received to reduce gradually the amount by which the cost of the bond exceeds its face value.

Annuity—A contract, usually issued by an insurance company that provides an income for a specified period of time, such as a number of years or for life. (See also Variable Annuity.)

Appreciation—Increase in value of property; opposite to depreciation.

Arbitrage—The buying of stocks, bonds, or other securities in one market and selling them in another.

Asked Price—In the case of mutual fund shares, the price at which the buyer may purchase stock from the investment company; i.e., the net asset value per share plus the sales charge, if any. In the case of closed-end shares, the lowest price at which the stock is then offered for sale in the public market.

Asset(s)—(1) The property of a deceased person subject to the payments of his debts and gifts. (2) The property in a trust account.

Bearer Bonds—Bonds which are not registered as to the name of the owner but are the property of the holder and title to which passes by delivery.

Beneficiary—(1) The person for whose benefit a trust is created. (2) The person to whom the amount of an insurance policy or annuity is payable.

Bequest—A gift of personal property by will; a legacy.

Bid Price—In the case of open-end shares, the price at which the holder may redeem his shares; in most cases it is the current net asset value per share. In the case of closed-end shares, the highest price then offered for stock in the public market, which may be more or less than net asset value per share.

Blue Chip—The common stock of a large, well-known corporation with a relatively stable record of earnings and dividend payments over a period of many years.

Bond—A security representing debt—a loan from the bondholder to the corporation.

Book Value—(1) The price at which assets are carried on a financial statement. (2) The value of each share of common or capital stock based on the values at which the assets of a corporation are carried on its balance sheet. It is obtained by deducting from total assets all liabilities of the corporation and dividing the remainder by the number of shares outstanding.

Broker—A person in the business of effecting transactions in securities for the accounts of others, who receives a commission for his services. Closed-end investment company shares are usually bought and sold through brokers.

Call—An option contract that gives the holder the right to purchase a particular security from another person at a specified price during the term of the option, which may be any period of time but is rarely longer than six months and ten days. May be used either for speculative or "hedging" purposes.

Call Price—A term generally used in connection with preferred stocks and debt securities having a fixed claim. It is the price that an issuer must pay in order voluntarily to retire such securities. Often call price exceeds par or liquidating price.

Capital Gains (and Losses)—The difference between purchase price and selling price in the sale of assets. The computation is used primarily in tax computations.

Capital Gains Distribution—A distribution to investment company shareholders from net long-term capital gains realized by a "regulated investment company" on the sale of portfolio securities.

Cash Surrender Value—The cash value of a life insurance policy contract if redeemed before the death of the insured.

Certificates of Deposit—Generally short-term, interest-bearing negotiable certificates issued by commercial banks or savings and loan associations against funds deposited in the issuing institution.
—*Euro CDs*—Issued by foreign branches of U.S. banks or U.S. branches of foreign banks.

Closed-End Investment Company—An investment company with a relatively fixed amount of capital, whose securities are traded on a securities exchange or in the over-the-counter market, as are the securities of operating business corporations.

Commercial Paper—Short-term, unsecured promissory notes issued by corporations to finance short-term credit needs. Commercial paper is usually sold on a discount basis and has a maturity at the time of issuance not exceeding nine months.

Common Stock—A security representing ownership of a corporation's assets. The right of common stock to dividends and assets ranks after the requirements of bonds, debentures and preferred stocks. Generally, shares of common stock carry voting rights.

Common Stock Fund—An investment company whose portfolio consists primarily of common stocks. Such a company may at times take a defensive position in cash, bonds and other senior securities.

Compound Interest—Payment of interest on the unpaid interest (usually periodically added to the principal) in addition to payment on the original principal.

Convertible Securities—Securities carrying the right (either unqualified or under stated conditions) to exchange the security for other securities of the issuer. Most frequently applies to preferred stocks or bonds carrying the right to exchange for given amounts of common stock.

Corporate Fiduciary—A trust institution serving in a fiduciary capacity, such as executor, administrator, trustee, or guardian.

Coupon Bonds—Bonds to which are attached coupons representing the interest payments. As the interest becomes due the coupons are clipped and presented for payment.

Debenture—A bond secured only by the general credit of the corporation.

Default—With regard to a bond or promissory note, the failure to make a payment either of principal or interest as or when due.

Defensive Stock—A stock which, because of the nature of the business represented, is believed likely to hold up relatively well in declining markets.

Depository—A place where something is deposited, such as a safe deposit vault.

Direct Purchase Fund—A mutual fund whose shares are purchased directly from the fund at no, or a low, charge; investor generally must deal directly with the fund, rather than through an investment dealer or broker.

Discount on Securities—The amount or percentage by which a security (a bond or a share of stock) is bought or sold for less than its face or par value; opposed to premium on securities.

Dividend—A payment from income on a share of common or preferred stock.

Dollar Cost Averaging—An automatic capital accumulation method that provides for regular purchases of equal dollar amounts of securities and results in an average cost per share lower than the average price at which purchases are made.

Earnings—*per Common Share*—net income after all charges, including preferred dividend requirements, divided by the number of common shares outstanding. Net income does not include profits from the sale of securities.

—*per Preferred Share*—net income after all charges, including any prior preferred dividend requirements, divided by the number of preferred shares outstanding.

Equity—The residue of value for the owner of an asset remaining after deducting prior claims. The equity of a corporation may be divided into common shares alone or may include preferred shares as well. In calculating the equity of a common stock, preferred stock as well as debt must be deducted from total assets.

Equity Security—Technically, the term refers to all securities other than debt, but is used sometimes to denote common stocks alone or preferred stocks of a quality rendering them subject to market fluctuations similar to those of common stocks.

Estate—(1) The right, title, or interest which a person has in any property to be distinguished from the property itself, which is the subject matter of the interest. (2) The property of a decedent.

Estate Plan—A definite plan for the administration and disposition of one's property during one's lifetime and at one's death; usually set forth in a will and one or more trust agreements.

Estate Tax—A tax imposed on a decedent's estate as such and not on the distributive shares of the estate or on the right to receive the shares; to be distinguished from an inheritance tax.

Executor—An individual or a trust institution nominated in a will and appointed by a court to settle the estate of the testator. If a woman, she is an executrix.

Fiduciary—A person who is vested with legal rights and powers to be exercised for the benefit of another person.

Fixed Income Security—A preferred stock or debt security with a stated percentage or dollar income return.

Government Agency Issues—Debt securities issued by government-sponsored enterprises, federal agencies and international institutions. Such securities are not direct obligations of the Treasury but involve government sponsorship or guarantees.

Hedge—To offset. Also, a security that has offsetting qualities. Thus, one attempts to "hedge" against inflation by the purchase of securities whose values should respond to inflationary developments. Securities having these qualities are "inflation hedges."

Heir—A person who inherits real property; to be distinguished from next of kin and from distributee. An heir of the body is an heir in the direct line of the decedent. A son, for example, is the heir of the body of his father or mother.

Income—The returns from property, such as rent, interest, dividends, profits, and royalties; opposed to principal or capital.

Income Beneficiary—The beneficiary of a trust who is entitled to receive the income from it.

Income Fund—An investment company whose primary objective is current income.

Indenture—A mutual agreement in writing between or among two or more parties whereof usually each party has a counterpart or duplicate; originally so called because the parts were indented by a notched cut or line so that the two parts could be fitted together.

Individual Retirement Account—A tax-saving retirement program for individuals, established under the Employee Retirement Income Security Act of 1974.

Inheritance Tax—A tax on the right to receive property by inheritance; to be distinguished from an estate tax.

Intestate—(Adjective) (1) Without having made and left a valid will. (2) Not devised or bequeathed; not disposed of by will. (Noun) A person who dies intestate.

Investment Company—A corporation or trust through which investors pool their money to obtain supervision and diversification of their investments.

Joint Tenancy—The holding of property by two or more persons in such a manner that, upon the death of one joint owner, the survivor or survivors take the entire property; to be distinguished from tenancy in common and tenancy by the entirety.

Keogh Plan—A tax-saving retirement program for self-employed persons and their employees. (Also known as H.R. 10 Plans.)

Leverage—The effect of the use of borrowed money or other senior capital, magnifying changes in the assets and earnings available for junior issues.
—*Effective*—Ratio obtained by dividing total assets working for a share of common stock by the market price of the stock.

Living Trust—A trust that becomes operative during the lifetime of the settlor; opposed to a trust under will. The same as a trust inter vivos.

Living Trust—A trust instrument made effective during the lifetime of the creator; in contrast to a Testamentary Trust, which is created under a will.

Management Investment Company—A broad term covering all mutual funds and closed-end investment companies which change their portfolio holdings from time to time. The exceptions are a few funds that have fixed lists of holdings, and contractual plans; these are defined by the Investment Company Act as "unit investment trusts."

Maturity—The date on which the principal of a bond or note becomes due and payable.

Money Market Fund—A mutual fund whose investments are primarily, or exclusively, in short-term debt securities, designed to maximize current income with liquidity and capital preservation.

Municipal Bonds—Bonds issued by public authorities—particularly the political subdivisions within the states, such as a city or county.

Municipal Bond Fund—Unit investment trust or open-end company whose shares represent diversified holdings.

Mutual Fund—Same as Open-End Investment Company.

No-Load Fund—See Direct Purchase Fund.

Non-Callable Bond—A bond that cannot, under the terms of the issue, be called by the obligor (the corporation) for redemption or conversion.

Odd Lot—Less than a round lot, which is usually 100 shares. On securities exchanges, buying and selling costs may be somewhat higher on odd lots than on round lots. Not applicable to open-end investment companies.

Open-End Investment Company—An investment company whose shares are redeemable at any time at approximate asset value. In most cases, new shares are offered for sale continuously.

Par Value—The face value of stocks and bonds.

Pension Plan—A retirement program based on a definite formula which provides fixed benefits to be paid to employees for their lifetime upon the attainment of a stated retirement age.

Power of Attorney—A document, witnessed and acknowledged, authorizing the person named therein to act as his agent, called attorney-in-fact, for the person signing the document. If the attorney-in-fact is authorized to act for his principal in all matters, he has a general power of attorney; if he has authority to do only certain specified things, he has a special power of attorney.

Preferred Stock—An equity security (generally carrying a fixed dividend) whose claim to earnings and assets must be paid before common stock is entitled to share.

Probate (Verb)—To present a will to the court for appointment of the executor or administrator c.t.a., which is the first step in the settlement of an estate.

Prospectus—The official document which describes the shares of a new security issue and must be supplied to each purchaser, under the Securities Act of 1933. Applies to mutual funds; to closed-end companies only when new capital is raised.

Proxy Statement—A written power of attorney that stockholders give to another person to vote their stock if they are not present at a stockholders' meeting.

Prudent Man Rule—The law governing the investment of trust funds in those states, now greatly in the majority, that give broad discretion to the trustee.

Put—An option contract that gives the holder the right to sell a particular security to another person at a specified price during the term of the option, which may be any period of time but is rarely longer than six months and ten days. May be used either for speculative or "hedging" purposes.

Registered Bond—A bond whose negotiability is withdrawn by a writing thereon that it belongs to a specified person, and by a registry to that effect at a specified date.

Remainderman—The person who is entitled to an estate after the prior estate has expired. For example, "I devise Blackacre to A for life, remainder to B." A is the life tenant; B, the remainderman. Originally the term applied, and in most states still does apply, to real property only.

Round Lot—A fixed unit of trading (usually 100 shares) to which prevailing commission rates on a securities exchange will apply.

Short Sale—The sale of a security which is not owned, in the hope that the price will go down so that it can be repurchased at a profit. The person making a short sale borrows stock in order to make delivery to the buyer and must eventually purchase the stock for return to the lender.

Sinking Fund—An accumulation of amounts set aside periodically by municipalities or corporations, which will be sufficient to satisfy a debt, such as a bond issue, at maturity.

Stock Split—The division of shares of stock of a corporation which goes to increase the number of outstanding shares but does not increase the capitalization of the company.

Stock Yield—The rate of return on a stock based upon its market value as of a particular date and the dividend being currently paid by the company.

Tenancy by the Entirety—Tenancy by a husband and wife in such a manner that, except in concert with the other, neither husband nor wife has a disposable interest in the property during the lifetime of the other. Upon the death of either, the property goes to the survivor. To be distinguished from joint tenancy and tenancy in common.

Tenancy in Common—The holding of property by two or more persons in such a manner that each has an undivided interest which, upon his death, passes as such to his heirs or devisees and not to the survivor or survivors; the same as an estate in common; to be distinguished from joint tenancy and tenancy by the entirety.

Testamentary Trust—A trust established by the terms of a will.

Testator—A man who has made and left a valid will at his death.

Total Return—A statistical measure of performance reflecting the result of acceptance of capital gains in shares, plus the result of reinvestment of income dividends.

Treasury Bill—Non-interest-bearing discount security issued by U.S. Treasury to finance the national debt. Most bills are issued to mature in 3 months, 6 months, or one year.

Trust—A fiduciary relationship in which one person (the trustee) is the holder of the legal title to property (the trust property) subject to an equitable obligation (an obligation enforceable in a court of equity) to keep or use the property for the benefit of another person (the beneficiary).

Trustee—An individual or a trust institution which holds the legal title to property for the benefit of someone else.

Unit Trust—An investment company, or contractual plan, which has a fixed portfolio.

U.S. Government Securities—Various types of marketable securities issued by the U.S. Treasury, which consist of bills, notes and bonds. Such securities are direct obligations of the U.S. Government and differ mainly in the length of their maturity. Treasury bills, the most frequently issued marketable government security, have a maturity of up to one year and are issued on a discount basis.

Variable Annuity—An annuity contract under which the dollar payments received are not fixed but fluctuate more or less in line with average common stock prices.

Variable Life Insurance—A contract or plan under which the death benefit and cash fluctuate in tandem with the investment performance of a Separate Account generally composed of common stock.

Volatility—The relative rate at which a security or fund share tends to move up or down in price. Is usually measured by comparing percentage changes in the price of a stock with those in a market average, such as the New York Stock Exchange Common Stock Index, between the same dates. For example, if the asset value of a fund advanced 15 per cent while the NYSE Index rose 10 per cent, the volatility of the fund would be 15 divided by 10 or 1.50.

Warrant—An option to buy a specified number of shares of the issuing company's stock at a specified price. The warrant may be valid for a limited period of time only, or it may be valid permanently.

Will—A legally enforceable declaration of a person's wishes in writing regarding matters to be attended to after his death and inoperative until his death. A will usually, but not always, relates to the testator's property, is revocable (or amendable by means of a codicil) up to the time of his death, and is applicable to the situation which exists at the time of his death.

Yield—Income received from investments, usually expressed as a percentage of market price; also referred to as return.

Yield to Maturity—Rate of return on a debt security held to maturity; both interest payments and capital gain or loss are taken into account.

Index

136